Soups & Sauces

DAVID & CHARLES

Newton Abbot London

British Library Cataloguing in Publication Data
Soups & sauces.—(David & Charles Kitchen Workshop)
   1. Soups   2. Sauces
   I. Supper og sauser. *English*
   641.8'13   TX757

ISBN 0-7153-8458-9

Filmset by MS Filmsetting Ltd, Frome, Somerset
and printed in The Netherlands
by Smeets Offset BV, Weert
for David & Charles (Publishers) Limited
Brunel House, Newton Abbot, Devon

Soups and Sauces

Soups and sauces have so much in common that it is only natural to give recipes for them in the same book. The primary basis of most soups and sauces is a good stock, and in the following pages we tell you how to make a stock from meat, fish, poultry and vegetables.

Soups

Whether served cold or hot, soups are tasty and filling as well as fairly economical. A good soup can be served either as a starter, as a meal in its own right – or even as a dessert – depending on its ingredients, whether it is thick or thin in consistency, clear or thickened. If you are serving an expensive main course, for instance, it is wise to serve soup as a starter, because it is filling, thus making the main course stretch to serve more portions. You must also always consider the relationship in taste and texture between your soups and the other courses of a meal.

One of the greatest advantages of most soups is that they can be made in advance and just re-heated before serving, and furthermore, many soups can be very happily frozen. As with casseroles, you can make a large quantity of soup at one go, and freeze half for a later emergency or family meal.

Many busy cooks like to use canned or packeted soups. These are easy to prepare and often very tasty, but try always to give them your own personal touch, by adding spices, herbs, cream, finely chopped mushrooms etc.

Broadly speaking, soups fall into two main groups – thick and thin. Clear soups, which consist of consommés and homely broths, are made with very good meat stocks, and are served without being sieved or liquidized. Thickened soups may be thickened in various ways – with a flour and butter roux or a starch such as potato flour, arrowroot or cornflour; with the starchy purée of a vegetable like potato; or very often with a liaison of cream and egg yolk. Cream soups are basically vegetable, fish or poultry purées thickened with a béchamel or velouté sauce

4

(see page 13) and enriched at the last moment with cream.

Stock

A good meat stock is the basis for most soups. You can just use bones, with some meat still attached, or include some cheaper cuts of meat as well, to give a wonderful flavour. Make white stock with poultry or veal, fish stock with bones, skin and trimmings off fish fillets, or brown stock from beef or veal bones, browned first in the pan or in the oven.

Instead of stock you can always use stock cubes with water, as directed on the packet. In most recipes use chicken stock cubes, as their milder flavour does not dominate other ingredients.

Meat Stock

For each kg (about 2¼lb) of bones and meat, allow about 1½ litres (2½–2¾pt) water and 1–2 × 5ml tsp (1–2tsp) salt. Rinse bones and meat if necessary and chop up, or saw larger bones into smaller pieces (the smaller the pieces, the better the stock, as maximum surface of bones and meat is exposed, thus adding goodness and flavour to the liquid). Place everything in a large pot and add cold water (*not* hot). Bring slowly to the boil and skim well. This is vital to make the stock clear. (You may have to skim again during the simmering.) Add flavourings like onions, carrots, celery, leek, bay leaves, parsley, peppercorns etc.

Add salt and cover the pot. Leave stock to simmer for at least 2½–3hr (*never* boil it, as this causes scum to combine with any fat). Remove meat and bones and strain broth, several times if necessary. Any meat left on the bones can be cut off and used in another dish – or indeed in the soup itself – but remember that nearly all the nourishment and flavour have gone into the stock. If you are going to use the stock as a clear soup or consommé, strain off the fat. The simplest way of doing this is to cool the stock, then cool further in the refrigerator, when the fat solidifies into a white lid on the surface which can be simply lifted off.

If you want a stock that will jell, to make aspic or jellied consommé, for instance, you must use veal knuckle which contains lots of gelatine. Next best is beef knuckle (fish bones too contain gelatine). These stocks should be skimmed, reduced and cleared meticulously. To clear stock, remove as much of the fat as possible and pour stock into a clean pot. Whisk 2–3 raw egg whites per 1 litre (1¾pt) stock lightly together. Crush a few washed egg shells. Add both the egg whites and the shells to the cold stock. Bring slowly to the boil, whisking only until the mixture looks milky. Then stop whisking,

5

and leave to simmer, and the egg shells and whites will rise gradually to the top of the pot, the coagulated egg white having trapped the tiny particles or impurities which cloud the stock. Leave to simmer quietly for about 30 min, and strain.

Chicken or Poultry Stock

The best chicken stock of all comes from a fresh boiling fowl, but you can use the carcase of a cooked bird. Slice or chop up carcase (with skin and giblets) or fowl, and put in a pot. Add water until contents are covered and bring to the boil. Skim. Add 1–2 scraped and washed carrots, 1 large leek, 1 onion and $\frac{1}{2}$ sprig of parsley. Add 2 × 5ml tsp (2tsp) salt and 8–10 black peppercorns and bring to the boil. Skim when it boils, and immediately turn down heat. Simmer for at least 2–3 hr. Strain and cool off the stock. Remove any fat.

Vegetable Stock

When making vegetable soups the vegetables are usually boiled in water which is used as the basis for the soup. If you want a really tasty stock, allow scraped and washed, sliced vegetables to sauté for a while in butter before adding water.

Never waste the peelings or trimmings of vegetables – such as the outer cabbage leaves or stems, cauliflower stalks, the green top of the leek, celery tops and leaves etc – as they all contribute flavour to stock.

Place the vegetables in boiling, lightly salted water and leave to simmer until everything is tender. Add salt if you are using the broth immediately, but if you want to freeze it, only season when you want to use it.

Fish Stock

Never leave the fishmonger without the heads, bones and trimmings of your filleted white fish, as it makes very good stock for fish soups and casseroles, for fishy sauces, or for poaching fish fillets for use in a recipe (see below).

Clean and wash fish heads, trimmings and bones. Place in a large pot and add enough water to cover contents. Bring to the boil on low heat and skim well. Add a couple of small onions, salt, a few sprigs of dill, parsley and a bay leaf, and a few white peppercorns. Leave broth to simmer on low heat for 20–30 min. If you've cooked your fish at the same time, remove and use in recipe, then strain the stock.

Freezing Stock

Put stock in rigid plastic containers or freezer bags (inside a rigid container until frozen). Remember to write date and name on the packaging. Freeze quickly.

Straining and Freezing Stock

1 Strain stock through either a clean piece of muslin or other form of filter placed in a colander or sieve.

2 Remove fat from hot stock with paper kitchen towel. When stock is cold the fat can be blotted up by placing several layers of folded paper kitchen towel on top of the stock.

3 The cold fat-free stock is poured into strong freezer bags inside rigid plastic containers. When frozen, the bags can be removed and closed securely, and easily stored in the freezer.

Thickening Soups

To thicken simply means to make a thin liquid somewhat thicker and smoother in consistency. You can do this in several ways.

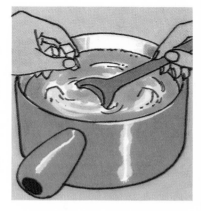

Vegetable Thickening
1 A special drum sieve is the best utensil for this purpose as its mesh is so fine. Use a wooden pestle or a stiff rubber scraper to force the vegetables through.

2 An ordinary sieve is almost as good. Place across a bowl and push vegetables through with a wooden spoon or pestle.

Butter and Flour Thickening
Mix together equal amounts of soft butter and plain flour. Shape into nuts or balls and stir or whisk, a little at a time, into the boiling liquid.

Egg and/or Cream Thickening
1 Whisk some of the hot soup into the egg yolk and/or cream mixture.

2 Add thickening to soup, whisking continuously, and keep the soup just below boiling point.

3 Pour the soup once cooked into an attractive serving bowl, take to the table, and ladle into plates or bowls.

Flour Thickening

Plain flour, cornflour, potato flour or arrowroot can be mixed with cold water or stock. Stir until free of lumps, then add to boiling soups or sauces, stirring vigorously. Plain flour and cornflour are used in soups and sauces. Bring to a boil and then leave to simmer for a few minutes to get rid of the taste of raw flour. Potato flour, cornflour or arrowroot are used in fruit or dessert soups, and also in soups and sauces where the colour and clarity are important. Mix flour with cold water and add to the soup, stirring vigorously. Do *not* allow to boil, and remove pot from heat the minute it begins to do so.

Vegetable Purée Thickening

Vegetables and potatoes boiled in the stock are often used to thicken cream soups and sauces. The vegetables are mashed through a sieve as shown in the small illustrations opposite. Or you can purée them in a liquidizer: put vegetables and some of the stock in the liquidizer goblet and run at top speed for a few seconds. Put the purée back into the stock and heat the soup or the sauce thoroughly before serving.

Egg and/or Cream Thickening

You can use egg yolks and/or cream to thicken your soup or sauce. This will give a nice, rich flavour. Whisk egg yolks lightly, with or without cream, and stir in some of the hot broth. Whisk this back into the soup or the sauce.

NOTE Do *not* allow the soup or sauce to boil after you have added this thickening, otherwise the egg may curdle.

Butter and Flour Thickening

There are two ways of thickening soups and sauces using butter and flour.

● Mix soft butter with an equal amount of plain flour to make a smooth paste – called beurre manié. Shape into little nuts or balls, and whisk into the hot liquid. Stir. It will dissolve and thicken the broth while the soup or sauce is simmering.

● Melt butter in a pot and stir in the plain flour. Allow thickening to simmer on low heat for a few minutes without letting it go brown. Add boiling liquid gradually, stirring all the while.

Good Basic Sauces

You can make a fairly simple dish into something special just by serving it with a tasty sauce or gravy. As a result many dishes are named after the sauce which is served with them. There are an incredible number of different recipes for sauces, but most of them are made from the basic three 'mother' sauces – white or béchamel, velouté, and brown.

White or Béchamel Sauce. This is the most basic and most common of all sauces, and is made from butter, plain flour and milk, seasoned to taste with salt and white pepper, with perhaps a few flavourings added (see page 13).

Velouté Sauce. The difference between this and béchamel is that it is made with stock – vegetable, chicken, veal or fish – instead of milk.

Brown Sauce. This is made by *browning* butter and plain flour, and then adding brown stock or meat juices. To get a really brown sauce, brown the butter and the flour until it is the colour of dark, plain chocolate. Dilute with a good brown stock and serve with dark meat with a strong flavour, beef for instance.

To get a medium brown sauce, brown the butter and the flour for less time, just until the colour resembles milk chocolate. Dilute with a lighter meat stock and serve with lighter meats, veal and pork for instance.

Other basic types of sauce are the egg yolk and butter sauces – hollandaise, béarnaise etc – and the egg yolk and oil sauces, the 'mother' of which is mayonnaise. The latter is

always served cold, the former are mostly served warm, and the use of a bain marie or water bath is vital to keep them warm, or indeed to cook them. Use a roasting tin half-filled with hot water for several pans at a time, or a pan with a bowl fitting into it so that the bowl is kept hot by the water beneath (which must not touch the bottom of the bowl).

Flavouring Sauces
A good basic sauce should be smooth with no lumps (sieve them away if necessary), and seasoned to taste with salt and pepper. Always simmer the sauce until the flour taste is cooked off.

White or Béchamel Sauce.
This basic sauce (see next page) with various flavourings added, becomes classic French coating sauces – Crème (with cream), Mornay (with cheese), Poulette (with shallots, mushrooms, egg yolks and cream), Ravigote (with white wine, onions and herbs), and Soubise (with onion purée) – or the base of savoury soufflés and cream soups. You can also flavour white sauces with anchovy essence, tomato purée, chopped herbs such as dill, parsley, tarragon and capers, and with curry

powder and mustard (use coarse Moutarde de Meaux for a more interesting texture).

When making a curry sauce, sauté the curry powder with the butter before adding the flour, for the best flavour. The same applies to paprika, but never allow the paprika to brown, as it gives a burnt flavour.

When using grated cheese to flavour your sauce, it must not be allowed to boil as this will make it stringy and sticky. Cheddar is one of the best cooking cheeses.

Velouté Sauce.
This 'mother' sauce is the basic of Aurore (with tomato), Bercy (white wine and shallots), Normande (with white wine, for fish), and Suprême (with cream).

Brown Sauce.
This third basic sauce becomes, with various additions, the classic French sauce Bourgignonne (with red wine, mushrooms and onions), Chasseur (with white wine, mushrooms and shallots), Duxelles (with mushrooms), Lyonnaise (with onions and white wine), Piquante (with white wine, pepper, pickle and capers) and Venison (with pepper, redcurrant jelly and cream).

Tasty Sauces

BASIC BROWN SAUCE (Espagnole)

25–40g (1–1½oz) butter
1 carrot
1 onion, ½ stalk celery
2 × 15ml tbsp (2tbsp) plain flour
1 litre (1¾pt) good brown stock
1 sprig of parsley, 1 sprig of thyme, 1 bay leaf

Grate carrot, and finely chop the onion and celery. Melt the butter and sauté vegetables until lightly golden. Stir in flour and leave until everything has a nice, even, brown colour. Dilute with hot stock and add thyme, parsley and bay leaf when sauce is smooth. Leave to simmer without a lid for about 30 min, until it has reduced by about ⅓, and strain. This sauce can be frozen.

VARIATIONS
Sauce Bordelaise
Add 100ml (4fl oz) red wine and 1 finely chopped shallot to ½ litre (just under 1pt) basic brown sauce, and simmer until it has reduced by half. Add finely chopped parsley. Serve with grilled steaks, for instance.

Sauce Chasseur
Sauté 1 finely chopped shallot and 100g (4oz) finely chopped mushrooms in butter, and then simmer until tender in 150ml (¼pt) white wine. Add, with 1 × 15ml tbsp (1tbsp) tomato purée to ½ litre (just under 1 pt) basic brown sauce. Add finely chopped parsley as a final touch. Serve with grills and roasts.

BASIC WHITE SAUCE (Béchamel)

25–40g (1–1½oz) butter
3 finely chopped or grated shallots
½ stalk celery
2 × 15ml tbsp (2tbsp) plain flour
½ litre (just under 1 pt) warm milk
1 sprig of thyme, 1 bay leaf, 6 peppercorns

Sauté shallots and celery in butter without allowing it to go brown. Stir in flour and dilute with warm milk, a little at the time. Place thyme, bay leaf and peppercorns in the sauce and leave to simmer for about 15–20 min. Strain sauce before ser-

ving. You could also, if you wish the sauce to be more subtly flavoured, add the seasoning ingredients – celery, shallots, herbs and peppercorns – to the milk before you heat it. Leave to infuse for 5–7 min, before straining, and using in sauce.

VARIATIONS
You can vary the white sauce by adding finely chopped parsley, sautéed onion, tomato purée, grated horseradish or cheese. A dash of cream will round off both the taste and the consistency. Serve with vegetables, fish, chicken and eggs.

BASIC VELOUTÉ SAUCE

25–40g (1–1½oz) butter
2 × 15ml tbsp (2tbsp) plain flour
½ litre (just under 1pt) white stock

Melt the butter and stir in plain flour. Allow mixture to sauté for a few minutes, but do not allow it to go brown. Dilute with warm stock and leave to simmer for about 10 min. Serve the sauce either as it is or add finely chopped parsley, grated horseradish, spinach or dill.

VARIATIONS
Lemon Sauce
Make the basic velouté sauce as above, but with 400ml (¾pt) stock. Season sauce to taste with 100ml (4fl oz) cream, juice of 1 lemon, 1 × 15 ml tbsp (1tbsp) finely chopped parsley, salt and pepper. Serve with poultry, fish and lamb.

Onion Sauce
Make the basic velouté sauce as above, but sauté a small grated or finely chopped onion in the butter (do not allow to go brown) before you stir in the flour. Dilute with stock and season to taste with vinegar and sugar. This sauce goes particularly well with beef dishes.

Mustard Sauce
2 × 15ml tbsp (2tbsp) Dijon mustard
3 × 5ml tsp (3tsp) strong French mustard
2 × 15ml tbsp (2tbsp) sugar
1 egg yolk
150–200ml (5–7fl oz) oil
1 × 15ml tbsp (1tbsp) white wine vinegar
salt, white pepper
2 × 15ml tbsp (2tbsp) finely chopped dill

1 Whisk together mustards, sugar and egg yolk.
2 Add oil, first one drop at a time, and increase as you go along. Whisk vigorously all the time. Season to taste with vinegar, salt and white pepper, and stir in dill.
This sauce is one of the mayonnaise oil and egg yolk sauces, and its mustardy flavour goes well with smoked salmon or trout, with spiced herrings and shellfish.

Cream Sauce with Port and Walnuts (left)
This sauce is delicious with chicken, turkey and all kinds of game.

25g (1oz) butter
1 × 15ml tbsp (1tbsp) plain flour
300–400ml (½–¾pt) meat juices or good stock
about 100ml (4fl oz) double cream
about 100ml (4fl oz) port wine
50g (2oz) chopped walnuts
a little salt and pepper

1 Melt butter, stir in flour and allow to sauté for 3 min. Do not allow to go brown.
2 Dilute with meat juices or stock and cream until the sauce is the right consistency. Leave to simmer for 10 min. Add port and walnuts, and heat through. Season just before serving hot.

Sweet and Sour Sauce
1 finely chopped onion
1 finely shredded red pepper
1 × 15ml tbsp (1tbsp) oil
250ml (9fl oz) chicken stock
1–2 × 15ml tbsp (1–2tbsp) honey
1 × 15ml tbsp (1tbsp) soy sauce
1 × 15ml tbsp (1tbsp) white wine vinegar
1 chunk preserved ginger, finely chopped
1 × 15ml tbsp (1tbsp) cornflour

1 Sauté onion and pepper in oil, but do not allow to go brown. Stir the honey into the stock and pour mixture on top of vegetables. Add soy sauce, vinegar and ginger.
2 Stir cornflour into a little water and add to sauce to thicken it. Bring to boil and add more soy to taste.
This is the basic – and very useful – Chinese sweet and sour sauce, and it goes well with roast pork and chicken, deep-fried shrimps and any dish to be served with rice.

HOLLANDAISE SAUCE

3 egg yolks, 150g (5oz) butter
1 × 15ml tbsp (1tbsp) white wine
   vinegar or white wine
4 × 15ml tbsp (4tbsp) water
a pinch of white pepper
cayenne pepper
lemon juice

1 Melt the butter, skim, and allow to cool until tepid. Boil white pepper, vinegar and water together for about 5 min to reduce a little and strain through a fine filter.
2 Cool, then whisk egg yolks into the mixture.
3 Place saucepan in a bain marie over a low heat and whisk contents vigorously until the sauce goes thick.
4 Add melted, cooled butter gradually (a few drops at a time at first) to the sauce, whisking continuously. Season to taste with a dash of cayenne pepper and a few drops of lemon juice.
NOTE If the sauce curdles, remove at once from the heat. Start the sauce again. Whisk 1 egg yolk and 1 × 15ml tbsp (1tbsp) water together vigorously. Gradually whisk in the curdled sauce a little at the time, drop by drop. If, however, the sauce is so curdled that it is granular, it should be discarded.

VARIATIONS
Sauce Venetienne
1 portion Hollandaise Sauce
3 × 15ml tbsp (3tbsp) finely chopped
   onion
1–2 × 15ml tbsp (1–2tbsp) white
   wine vinegar
1 × 15ml tbsp (1tbsp) finely chopped
   tarragon and chervil
100ml (4fl oz) white wine
100ml (4fl oz) water

Vegetable Sauce (above)
1 onion, 1 clove of garlic
1 sprig of parsley
oil, salt
freshly ground pepper
25g (1oz) breadcrumbs
300–400ml ($\frac{1}{2}$–$\frac{3}{4}$pt) good stock
25–40g (1–1$\frac{1}{2}$oz) grated cheese
   (Cheddar)

1 Peel onion and garlic and chop finely. Wash parsley, dry it well and chop finely. Sauté onion, garlic and parsley in a little oil for 5 min on low heat.
2 Add salt, pepper and breadcrumbs. Stir in boiling stock until the sauce reaches the right consistency. Add grated cheese. This sauce is delicious with boiled vegetables. Serve hot.
1

Hollandaise Sauce (below)
1 After melting the butter, boil vinegar or white wine, water and pepper for a few minutes, strain and cool.
2 Pour mixture back into pot and whisk in the egg yolks.
3 Place pot in a water bath or bain marie (the water should not be boiling), and whisk vigorously until it thickens.
4 Add melted, cooled butter. Stir into the sauce, a little at the time, whisking vigorously and continuously. Start with a few drops and increase gradually.

Hollandaise is the classic sauce to serve with salmon, vegetables, asparagus, certain meats and fish. Mix in 100ml (4fl oz) stiffly whipped double cream for Sauce Mousseline.
2

3

Mix onion, herbs, vinegar, white wine and water together, and boil until liquid has reduced by $\frac{1}{4}$. Leave to cool and whisk into the Hollandaise Sauce. This goes well with fish.

Sauce Béarnaise

200g (7oz) butter
3 egg yolks
2 × 15ml tbsp (2tbsp) water
salt, pepper, lemon juice
3–4 × 15ml tbsp (3–4tbsp) chopped tarragon, parsley, chervil
For the spiced vinegar:
4 × 15ml tbsp (4tbsp) white wine
4 × 15ml tbsp (4tbsp) tarragon vinegar
2 shallots
10 white peppercorns
1 × 15ml tbsp (1tbsp) fresh tarragon or 1 × 15ml tsp (1tsp) dried
2–3 sprigs of parsley

1 To make the spiced vinegar, boil the wine and vinegar in a small saucepan with the shallots, crushed peppercorns, tarragon and parsley until reduced by about $\frac{2}{3}$. Strain and cool.
2 Melt the butter, skim and cool to tepid.
3 Whisk egg yolks with water and reduced vinegar in a bowl in a water bath until it thickens. (The water must not be boiling.)
4 Remove bowl from the heat and add the melted butter, a few drops at a time at first, and whisk until the sauce is thick and fluffy.
5 Season to taste with finely chopped herbs, salt, pepper and a little lemon juice.
NOTE If the sauce curdles you can whisk in an ice cube, 1–2 × 5ml tsp (1–2tsp) ice-cold water, or see note following Hollandaise Sauce recipe.
4

Sauce Choron (above)

This sauce goes just as well with steak as it does with chicken, fish and eggs. Basically it is a béarnaise sauce with a flavouring of tomato.

175g (6oz) butter
1 × 5ml tsp (1tsp) finely chopped onion
4 × 15ml tbsp (4tbsp) white wine vinegar
5 egg yolks, salt, pepper
2 × 15ml tbsp (2tbsp) meat juices or good, strong stock
100ml (4fl oz) tomato purée
cayenne pepper

1 Melt butter, skim, and cool.
2 Mix onion, a little salt and pepper, and vinegar in a saucepan and boil until reduced by about $\frac{1}{3}$.
3 Cool, then vigorously whisk egg yolks into sauce over a very low heat or in a water bath (bain marie). Remove saucepan from heat and whisk in melted, cooled butter and meat juices or stock alternatively, a few drops at a time.
4 Strain sauce through a sieve and add tomato purée and a tiny pinch of cayenne. Taste for seasoning, and reheat in a bain marie, but take care as it curdles very easily.

Cold Sauces

Fish, meat and vegetables are often served with cold sauces, which add both taste and visual appeal. They make interesting party dips, too.

Cocktail Sauce

*5–6 × 15ml tbsp (5–6tbsp)
   mayonnaise
100ml (4fl oz) plain yoghurt
1–2 × 15ml tbsp (1–2 tbsp) lemon
   juice
½ × 5ml tsp (½tsp) Tabasco sauce
salt, pepper, paprika
4–5 × 15ml tbsp (4–5tbsp) tomato
   purée
100ml (4fl oz) double cream*

1 Mix yoghurt and mayonnaise well together and season to taste with lemon juice, Tabasco, salt, pepper and paprika. Mix in tomato purée and stir well.
2 Whip cream until stiff and mix with the sauce. Taste, and season further if necessary.
Serve with all sorts of strongly flavoured meat dishes, poached fish or vegetables.

Curry Sauce

*250ml (9fl oz) sour cream
lemon juice
2–3 × 15ml tbsp (2–3tbsp) milk
salt, curry powder, turmeric, onion
   salt or finely grated onion*

1 Stir sour cream with a little lemon juice and enough milk until mixture is smooth and has the right consistency. Add spices to taste, but go easy on the plain salt if you use onion salt. Turmeric doesn't give much flavour, but adds a nice colour.
Serve with grilled or poached fish, and lamb or pork dishes. Boiled rice is a good accompaniment.

Pepper Sauce

*4 × 15ml tbsp (4tbsp) mayonnaise
about 150ml (¼pt) plain yoghurt
1 × 5ml tsp (1tsp) tomato purée
salt, cayenne pepper
paprika
½ red and ½ green pepper*

1 Stir mayonnaise, yoghurt and tomato purée well together. Season to taste with salt, a dash of cayenne

(only a dash – it's very strong) and paprika.
2 Clean peppers and chop them very finely. Mix with sauce and add a dash of lemon juice, cream or milk if the sauce seems too thick. Garnish with small slices of green or red pepper.
This sauce goes well with roasted or fried pork and veal.

Caraway Mayonnaise

*2 egg yolks
1 × 15ml tbsp (1tbsp) white wine
   vinegar
1 × 5ml tsp (1tsp) mustard
1 × 5ml tsp (1tsp) salt
250ml (9fl oz) oil
1 × 15ml tbsp (1tbsp) caraway seeds
lemon juice*

Mix egg yolks well with vinegar, mustard and salt. Stir in the oil, drop by drop at first, and slowly increasing the quantity. The mayonnaise is ready when it is thick, shiny and smooth. Grind the majority of the caraway seeds in a mortar and mix into the mayonnaise. Season with lemon juice and sprinkle remaining whole caraway seeds on top to garnish.

Green Peppercorn Sauce

*4 × 15ml tbsp (4tbsp) cottage cheese
3 × 15ml tbsp (3tbsp) sour cream or
   yoghurt
½ × 5ml tsp (½tsp) salt
1 × 5ml tsp (1tsp) lemon juice
2 × 15ml tbsp (2tbsp) green
   peppercorns
a dash of vodka (optional)*

Mix together cottage cheese and sour cream or yoghurt. Season to taste with salt, lemon juice and a dash of vodka. Stir in crushed peppercorns, leaving a few whole to garnish the top.

Cucumber Sauce

*200ml (7fl oz) plain yoghurt
2 × 5ml tsp (2tsp) mustard
½ × 5ml tsp (½tsp) salt
a pinch of white pepper
1 small onion
100g (4oz) cucumber*

Mix together yoghurt, mustard, salt and pepper. Finely chop, grate or shred the onion and cucumber (with or without skin), and mix into the yoghurt.

Apple Curry Sauce

*about 100g (4oz) mayonnaise
2 × 15ml tbsp (2tbsp) cream
1 × 15ml tbsp (1tbsp) mango chutney
2 × 15ml tbsp (2tbsp) curry powder
½ × 5ml tsp (½tsp) salt
½ × 5ml tsp (½tsp) sugar
a pinch of ground ginger
lemon juice, 1 small apple*

Mix together all the ingredients except the apple. Peel apple, remove core and either grate it or chop very finely. Mix into the sauce and garnish with small cubes of apple if you like.

Green Herb Sauce

*250ml (9fl oz) plain yoghurt
250ml (9lf oz) cottage cheese
1 clove of garlic, lemon juice
salt, white pepper
finely chopped herbs (see below)*

1 Mix yoghurt with the cottage cheese and stir well. Add crushed garlic and season to taste with lemon juice, salt and pepper. Add finely chopped herbs that will suit the dish you are going to serve with this particular sauce. With fried or poached fish you can use parsley, dill, chives or lemon balm; with grilled or roasted meat, parsley, chervil or basil; with smoked meat, egg and vegetable dishes, chives, cress, chervil and basil.

4

1 *Green Herb Sauce.*
2 *Cucumber Sauce.*
3 *Caraway Mayonnaise.*
4 *Apple Curry Sauce.*
5 *Pepper Sauce.*
6 *Green Peppercorn Sauce.*

Seasonal Soups

*From fresh ingredients easily
available all year round, you
can make delicious soups for a
simple lunch, for a more
sophisticated dinner, or for an
easy and tasty snack.*

*Tasty soups galore, on this
and the following pages.
From left : Cauliflower Soup,
Onion Soup, Curry Soup,
Chicken Soup with Dumplings,
Green Pea Soup, and
Tomato Soup with Pasta.*

Tomato Soup with Pasta

(serves 4)
Preparation time: about 10 min
Cooking time: about 55 min
Suitable for the freezer without the pasta

25g (1oz) butter, 1 chopped onion
100g (4oz) tomato purée
1 whole clove
1 bay leaf
1 × 5ml tsp (1tsp) oregano
¼ × 5ml tsp (¼tsp) dried thyme
salt, pepper
1 litre (1¾pt) stock
100g (4oz) pasta (short-cut macaroni, shells etc)

1 Boil the pasta first in lightly salted water until *al dente* (still with a little crunch when you bite it). Rinse in cold water.

2 Melt butter in a saucepan, add chopped onion and sauté until transparent and soft. Add tomato purée and leave to simmer, stirring continuously. When the tomato purée starts to turn deep red, add spices, herbs, seasonings and stock. Leave soup to simmer, covered, for about 45 min. Strain, then pour back into saucepan.

3 Add the cooked pasta, reheat soup, and serve with a sprinkling of Parmesan cheese.

Curry Soup

(serves 4)
Preparation time: about 10 min
Cooking time: 25 min
Unsuitable for the freezer

1 medium onion
25g (1oz) butter
1 × 15ml tbsp (1tbsp) plain flour
2 × 15ml tbsp (2tbsp) curry powder
1 litre (1¾pt) chicken stock
100ml (4fl oz) coconut milk (see method)
nutmeg, salt
1 egg yolk
200ml (7fl oz) double cream

1 Peel and finely chop onion. Sauté in butter until transparent and shiny. Sprinkle with curry powder and leave to simmer on low heat for about 5 min before adding the flour.

2 Mix in the stock slowly, then leave soup to boil for 15 min. Strain.

3 Add coconut milk. If you can't get hold of a fresh coconut, you can make coconut milk yourself. Pour 100ml (4fl oz) boiling water over 50g (2oz) shredded, desiccated or creamed coconut. Leave to settle for 30 min, then strain through a sieve. Squeeze to get all the water out.

4 Season to taste with salt and a little freshly grated nutmeg, and thicken with the cream and egg yolk whisked together.

Serve soup hot, adding crisply fried bacon shreds if you like, as a garnish.

Cauliflower Soup

(serves 6)
Preparation time: about 10 min
Cooking time: 35–45 min in all
Suitable for the freezer

25g (1oz) butter, 1 large onion
  1 medium cauliflower
600ml (1pt) chicken stock
600 ml (1pt) milk
salt, white pepper
1 whole mace
1 bay leaf
150ml (¼pt) single cream
finely chopped parsley

1 Melt the butter, slice the peeled onion thinly, and sauté until soft and shiny. Clean and wash the cauliflower and divide into small florets. Sauté along with the onion for about 5 min.

2 Add stock and milk and bring to the boil. Add salt, pepper, whole nutmeg and bay leaf. Put the lid on and simmer for 30–40 min. Remove bay leaf and mace.

3 Push soup through a sieve or purée in a liquidizer. Season to taste and add the cream. Heat soup gently and serve sprinkled with parsley.

Onion Soup

(serves 6)
Preparation time: about 15 min
Cooking time: 30 min
Suitable for the freezer (without the bread), but will lose flavour

450g (1lb) onions
50g (2oz) butter
1 × 15ml tbsp (1tbsp) plain flour
1.4 litres (2½pt) stock, salt, pepper
2 bay leaves
6 slices of toasted French bread
grated Gruyère or Parmesan cheese

1 Cut onions into thin rings and sauté in butter. Do not allow to go brown, and stir continuously. Sprinkle with flour and mix in, before adding the stock, bay leaves, salt and pepper. Leave to simmer for 30 min, then remove bay leaves and season further if necessary.
2 Pour soup into a large ovenproof dish or divide between 6 small ovenproof dishes. Place slices of toast on top and sprinkle with grated cheese. Quickly place under a hot grill to melt the cheese. Serve piping hot.

Chicken Soup with Dumplings

(serves 4)
Preparation time: 30–40 min
Cooking time: about 1 hr in all
Both soup and dumplings can be frozen separately

For the soup: 1 large boiling fowl
1.4 litres (2½pt) chicken stock (or water and 2 stock cubes)
1 egg white and egg shell
¼ celeriac or 2 stalks celery, 2 leeks
3 carrots
finely chopped parsley
salt, pepper
For the dumplings: 100g (4oz) raw breast meat from the chicken
1 egg white
100ml (4fl oz) double cream
salt, nutmeg

1 Make the dumplings first. Take the breast meat from the bird, and mince it a couple of times. Chill in the refrigerator. Mix in the cream, a little at a time, and season with salt and freshly grated nutmeg. Shape dough into small dumplings with a spoon and boil for a few minutes in lightly salted water.
2 To make the soup, place bird in a saucepan and pour the chicken stock over it. Boil slowly until bird is tender (about 40 min).
3 Remove bird, cool and use the meat the next day, in a chicken salad, for instance. (You could also freeze the meat for use later.)
4 Leave chicken broth to cool, whisk in 1 egg white with the crushed egg shell and heat to boiling point. Strain soup through a sieve used with muslin or fine clean cloth. Cube all the vegetables and add to soup. Boil until tender, about 20 min. Heat dumplings in the soup and serve warm, with bread.

VARIATION
To make the soup stretch further, you could add flour dumplings. Melt 50g (2oz) butter, add 50g (2oz) flour and then stir in with 100ml (4fl oz) water. Stir this dough over the heat until it leaves the sides of the pan. Season to taste with a pinch of freshly grated nutmeg. Whisk 2 eggs together, and add a little at the time. The dough must not be too thin, as you want to be able to shape it with a spoon. Shape small dumplings and boil in lightly salted water for a couple of min. Unsuitable for the freezer.

Carrot and Rice Soup

(serves 4)
Preparation time: 10–15 min
Cooking time: about 40 min
Unsuitable for the freezer

50g (2oz) bacon or fresh belly of pork
50g (2oz) butter
1 leek (white part only)
1 litre (1¾pt) stock
100g (4oz) round grain rice
450g (1lb) carrots, 1 large onion
salt, pepper, Worcestershire sauce

1 Cut belly of pork or bacon into cubes and fry lightly in ½ the butter. Clean leek, and slice the white part thinly. Add to the pan, with the stock, and bring to the boil. Remove the bacon or pork.
2 Carefully stir in the rice, cover the saucepan, and leave soup to simmer for about 30 min. Push soup through a sieve or liquidise and pour back into saucepan.
3 Scrape or peel the carrots, and grate them into the soup. Simmer for about 10 min. Season to taste with salt, pepper and Worcestershire sauce.

4 Peel onion, slice into thin rings, and fry until golden brown in remaining butter. Pour the hot soup into small bowls and garnish with fried onion rings.

Chicken Broth with Spaghetti

(serves 4)
Preparation time: 5–10 min
Cooking time: about 15 min
Unsuitable for the freezer

1 litre (1¾pt) chicken stock
1 red pepper
75g (3oz) frozen peas
75g (3oz) spaghetti
100g (4oz) cooked chicken
a pinch of saffron or turmeric
¼ × 5ml tsp (¼tsp) grated nutmeg
salt, pepper
2 × 15ml tbsp (2tbsp) finely chopped cress

1 Clean pepper and cube. Bring stock to the boil and add pepper cubes. Cover saucepan and leave soup to simmer for about 15 min.
2 Meanwhile boil spaghetti in plenty of lightly salted water and slice chicken meat finely. Add chicken meat, thawed peas and spaghetti to the soup and heat until nearly boiling. Season to taste.
3 Pour the soup into bowls, sprinkle generously with finely chopped cress and serve immediately.

Green Pea Soup

(serves 4)
Cooking time: 10 min
Unsuitable for the freezer

450g (1lb) frozen peas
1 litre (1¾pt) good strong stock (ham, perhaps)
2 egg yolks
150ml (4fl oz) single cream
salt, pepper
Worcestershire sauce
croûtons (see page 24)

1 Boil the frozen peas in the stock for about 10 min, then push through a sieve or use a liquidizer. Pour soup back into saucepan.
2 Reheat soup, but do not allow to boil. Season to taste with salt, pepper, Worcestershire sauce, and thicken with egg yolks whisked with cream. Do not let the soup boil after the egg yolks have been added. Serve soup piping hot, garnished with croûtons (see pages 24–5).

Tomato Soup with Shrimps

(serves 4)
Preparation time: 10 min
Cooking time: 20 min
Unsuitable for the freezer

1kg (2¼lb) tomatoes, 2 onions
50g (2oz) bacon or belly of pork
2 × 15ml tbsp (2tbsp) oil
1 × 15ml tbsp (1tbsp) plain flour
½ litre (just under 1pt) stock
salt, pepper
a pinch of sugar
¼ × 5ml tsp (¼tsp) celery salt
150g (5oz) peeled shrimps
parsley

1 Wash and dry the tomatoes and chop. Peel and chop up the onion. Cube bacon or belly of pork.
2 Heat the oil in a saucepan and add cubed meat and onion. Sauté until onion is shiny and soft. Sprinkle with flour and sauté everything for a couple of minutes without brown-ing. Add tomatoes and leave to simmer for 3 min, stirring continu-ously. Add stock, cover, and simmer for about 10–15 min.
3 Strain the soup through a fine-mesh sieve and season to taste with salt, pepper, celery salt and sugar. Add shrimps and heat soup, but do not allow to boil after shrimps have been added. Serve the soup im-mediately, garnished with parsley.

Vichyssoise

(serves 4)
Preparation time: 15 min
Cooking time: 30 min
Unsuitable for the freezer

3 leeks, 25g (1oz) butter
1 onion, 450g (1lb) potatoes
900ml (1½pt) chicken or veal stock
salt, pepper, grated nutmeg
1 egg yolk
150 ml (¼pt) double cream
finely chopped chives

Clockwise from top left: Carrot and Rice Soup, Tomato Soup with Shrimps, Vichyssoise, and Chicken Broth with Spaghetti.

1 Clean and wash the leeks. Remove most of the green parts, and slice the rest rest into thin rings. Peel onion and slice into thin rings.
2 Melt butter in a saucepan and sauté leek and onion for about 5 min. Do not allow to go brown.
3 Peel potatoes, cube, and add to the saucepan with the stock. Season to taste with salt, pepper and grated nutmeg. Leave soup on the boil for 30 min or until the potatoes are soft.
4 Push soup through a sieve or purée in a liquidizer. Pour soup back into the pan. Mix egg yolk with the cream and whisk misture into the soup. Heat soup, but do not bring to the boil. Season to taste once more and sprinkle with chives.
Serve soup hot or cold.

Clear or Thick Soups

When making a soup, you should consider first what you are serving in the same meal and when you are serving it. A clear soup, for instance, is ideal as a first course (see above), while a thickened or thicker soup can serve as a meal on its own (see left).

Clear Soups

The stock used is the most important constituent of a good, clear soup. This should always be specially made, by boiling bones as described in the introductory pages.

1 litre (1¾pt) stock will serve 4–5. In the picture above, a good clear chicken stock has been used to make a soup with vegetables, carrots, small sprigs of cauliflower, celery, chilli pepper, lemon slices and bay leaves. Any other vegetable could have been added: white cabbage, parsnip, celeriac, leek etc.

Place scraped, washed and chopped vegetables in boiling stock. They should all be cut to about the same size for ease of cooking. If you use frozen vegetable mixtures, add everything in one go. Boil on low heat until vegetables are tender, then season to taste. Sprinkle with parsley before serving.

Thickened Soups

The soup on the left has been thickened with round-grain rice. This is added to the stock and cooked until nearly ready before adding the sliced vegetables. Butter and flour, or flour alone, are also used to thicken soups. Dissolve the flour in some cold water, milk or cream and add to the soup, and cook for at least 5–10 min (to cook out the raw flour taste). You can also mix butter and flour (beurre manié) and drop little balls of this into the soup. Or you can start the whole operation by melting the butter, stirring in the flour, then diluting with boiling liquid, a little at a time (rather like making a velouté sauce). If you want a soup to be only slightly thickened, use an egg yolk. Whisk yolk lightly together with some of the broth and pour mixture into the soup. Never bring the soup back to the boil after adding egg yolks.

Soup Garnishes

A good soup is tasty enough on its own, but anything can always be enhanced by that little extra something!

Italian Courgette Soup (left)
(serves 4)
Preparation time: about 15 min
Cooking time: 10 min
Unsuitable for the freezer

1 kg (2¼lb) courgettes
2 × 15ml tbsp (2tbsp) finely chopped onion
15g (½oz) butter
1 × 15ml tbsp (1tbsp) oil
1 litre (1¾pt) chicken stock
salt, pepper
1 × 5ml tsp (1tsp) dried basil
2 egg yolks
40–50g (1½–2oz) grated Parmesan

1 Wash and peel the courgettes, and cut into cubes the size of sugar lumps.
2 Sauté courgettes and finely chopped onion in butter and oil, but do not brown. Add stock, seasonings, and herbs.
3 Leave soup to simmer for about 10 min on low heat or until the courgettes are soft. Whisk egg yolks with the cheese and pour mixture into the soup, stirring continuously. Do not bring back to the boil.
Season to taste and serve with croûtons (see below).

Croûtons

1 Cut white bread without crusts into even-sized cubes.

Petits Choux (Choux Puffs)

Preparation time: 10 min
Cooking time: about 20 min
Oven temperature: 240°C, 475°F,
Gas 9
Not suitable for the freezer

*150ml (¼pt) water, 50g (2oz) butter
50g (2oz) plain flour
2 small eggs*

1 Boil water and butter together in a
small saucepan. Add flour and stir
quickly until dough comes away
from the sides of the pan.
2 Leave dough to cool for a while,
then stir in the whisked eggs, a little
at a time, never adding more until
the last addition has been incorpo-
rated into the dough.
3 Pipe the dough out in small
mounds or spoons onto a greased
baking sheet. Bake in the hot oven
for about 20 min.
Leave the Petits Choux on a wire
rack to cool.
Slice off tops and fill with a cheese
cream, made from 100g (4oz) soft
butter, stirred together with 100g
(4oz) blue cheese.

Cheese Straws

Defrost frozen puff pastry at room
temperature. Roll out to whatever
thickness you prefer, slice in narrow
strips. Brush with egg white and
sprinkle generously with grated
cheese. Bake in the oven at about
220°C, 425°F, Gas 7 for about
20 min. These straws go well with
nearly all kinds of soups, and are
especially popular with children.

Cheese Tartlets

Defrost frozen puff pastry and
roll out. Press pastry into small
brioche or patty tins, and fill with
1 × 5ml tsp (1tsp) of the following:
75g (3oz) blue cheese, 25g (1oz)
butter, 1 egg and a pinch of paprika.
Bake tartlets at 200°C, 400°F, Gas 6
for 10–15 min.

*'Caviar' Bread is simplicity itself to
make, and makes this delicious
tomato soup with ham and vegetables
into a feast.*

Baked Cheese Sticks

Mix 50–60g (2–2½oz) butter with
about 50g (2oz) grated cheese,
2 × 15ml tbsp (2tbsp) cream and
1 × 15ml tbsp (1tbsp) brandy, if you
like. Spread cheese cream on white
bread slices, cut in long strips and
bake in oven for 8–10 min at about
250°C, 475°F, Gas 9. The surface
should be nice and brown. You can
also sprinkle the sticks with coarsely
chopped almonds or walnuts, which
have been quickly sautéed in a dry
frying pan.

'Caviar' Bread

Slice square white bread thinly, and
cut off crusts. Slice into triangles
and toast or fry in a little butter in
the frying pan.
Place triangular slices on top of each
other with lumpfish roe sandwiched
in between, and serve with the
piping hot tomato soup.

*2 Melt a little butter and oil in a
frying pan and fry bread cubes.*

*3 Fry on a very low heat, shaking the
pan to brown the cubes all over.*

Left: Rice Soup with Curry and Shrimps — a delicious, warming soup.

Right: Simple Onion Soup with Red Wine is satisfying, delicious, and very French.

700ml (1¼pt) stock or water + stock cube
1 can of tomatoes
1 small packet of frozen peas
200g (7oz) peeled shrimps
lemon, salt, pepper

1 Peel onions and leek and slice thinly. Sauté lightly in butter with curry powder and paprika.
2 Mix in the rice, simmer for a few moments, and then add liquid, the tomatoes with their juice, and the stock cubes (if using). Leave soup to simmer, covered, until rice is tender (about 20 min).
3 Add frozen peas and peeled shrimps. Heat soup, but do not bring back to the boil. Season to taste.
Serve with French bread or toast and butter.

Hot and Filling Soups

Plates of hot, filling soup are not only good for you – they can also be served as an impromptu meal or as a filling starter to an economical dinner.

Simple Onion Soup with Red Wine
(serves 4)
Preparation time: 15–20 min
Cooking time: about 20 min
Suitable for the freezer, without bread

4 large onions, 50g (2oz) butter
1 litre (1¾pt) water or stock
400ml (¾pt) red wine, pepper, salt
4 slices French bread
4 thick slices of cheese (Cheddar or Gruyère)
finely chopped parsley

1 Peel and cut onions into thin rings. Sauté in butter until golden.
2 Add water or stock and a little salt and pepper. Bring to the boil and skim if necessary. Leave soup to simmer on low heat until onion is tender, then add red wine, and season again to taste.
3 Pour soup into small ovenproof dishes or one large one. Float slices of bread with cheese and parsley on top and bake in a hot oven (240°C, 475°F, Gas 9) until the cheese has melted and is light gold in colour.

Rice Soup with Curry and Shrimps
(serves 4)
Preparation time: about 15 min
Cooking time: about 20 min
Unsuitable for the freezer

3 onions, 1 leek, butter
1 × 5ml tsp (1tsp) curry powder
½ × 5ml tsp (½tsp) paprika
100g (4oz) long-grain rice

Potato Soup with Sausages
(serves 4)
Preparation time: about 20 min
Cooking time: about 30 min
Unsuitable for the freezer

about 1kg (2¼lb) mealy potatoes
1 litre (1¾pt) stock or water
1½ × 5ml tsp (1½tsp) salt
½ × 5ml tsp (½tsp) pepper
500ml (just under 1pt) milk
1 onion, 25g (1oz) butter
finely chopped parsley
8 frankfurters

1 Peel potatoes, cube, and boil until tender in the stock or water.
2 Mash potatoes or purée in a liquidizer, and then mix with the stock in which they boiled, and the milk, and add sliced sausages. Heat soup and season to taste with salt and pepper. Fry onion rings in butter, then sprinkle over soup along with finely chopped parsley just before serving.
This potato soup is simple and hearty fare for a cold winter's day.

Vegetable Soup with Bacon
(right)
(serves 4)
Preparation time: 15–20 min
Cooking time: about 15 min

100g (4oz) bacon rashers
1 large onion, 4 stalks of celery
1 green pepper, 2 potatoes
1–2 bay leaves
250ml (9fl oz) stock
salt, white pepper
2½ × 15ml tbsp (2½tbsp) cornflour
1 litre (1¾pt) milk
1 can sweetcorn or 150g (5oz)
*   frozen sweetcorn*
finely chopped parsley

1 Chop the bacon rashers into strips and brown lightly in a large pan.
2 Coarsely chop the onion and slice celery. Cut cleaned pepper and peeled potatoes into slices or cubes.
3 Add onion, celery and pepper to the pan with the bacon and sauté for a few minutes. Add the potatoes, stock, bay leaves, salt and pepper. Leave soup to simmer for 10–12 min until potatoes are tender.
4 Mix cornflour with about 100ml (4fl oz) of the milk. Take saucepan off the heat and add milk thickening and the rest of the milk. Stir, and bring the soup back to boiling point.
5 Add drained or defrosted corn and leave soup to simmer for a couple of minutes. Season to taste, and sprinkle with finely chopped parsley just before serving.

Cabbage and Leek Soup (left)
(serves 4)
Preparation time: 15 min

150g (5oz) finely shredded white
*   cabbage*
2 leeks, 50g (2oz) butter
2 × 15ml tbsp (2tbsp) plain flour
1 litre (1¾pt) stock
3 × 15ml tbsp (3tbsp) tomato purée
2 × 5ml tsp (2tsp) caraway seeds
salt, white pepper
finely chopped parsley

1 Slice vegetables very finely and sauté in butter. Sprinkle with plain flour and then gradually add stock mixed with tomato purée.
2 Leave soup to simmer until vegetables are tender. Season with caraway seeds, salt and pepper. Sprinkle with finely chopped parsley and serve soup by itself, or with

homemade or canned meatballs. (See page 52 for a meatball recipe.) If you are using canned meatballs, use the stock from the tin as part of the stock when making the soup.

Tomato Soup with Vegetables
(serves 6)
For this soup you can follow the recipe for tomato soup on page 19, or use this one where we have used canned tomato soup. Add boiled vegetables. This soup is shown in the cover picture.
Preparation time: 5 min
Cooking time: a few minutes
Suitable for the freezer, but will lose flavour

2 cans of tomato soup (about 600ml
*   or 1pt)*
700ml (1¼pt) stock or water
100ml (4fl oz) single cream or top of
*   milk*
lemon juice
salt, pepper, paprika
3–4 × 15ml tbsp (3–4tbsp) sherry
*   (optional)*
2–3 drops of Tabasco sauce
300g (11oz) cooked, green beans
100g (4oz) cooked, sliced courgettes
*   or left-over cooked sweetcorn,*
*   peas, cauliflower, leek, celery etc*
sour cream or double cream
chives

Mix tomato soup with stock and cream or top of milk, and season to taste with lemon juice, salt, pepper and paprika. Heat thoroughly and add Tabasco and sherry (if used). Add the cooked vegetables and serve soup piping hot with a dollop of sour cream or double cream on top.

Green Soups

Spinach Soup
(serves 4)
Preparation time: 5 min + defrosting of spinach
Cooking time: about 5 min

225g (½lb) frozen spinach
25g (1oz) butter
1 × 15ml tbsp (1tbsp) plain flour
1 litre (1¾pt) stock
grated nutmeg
1–2 egg yolks
100ml (4fl oz) cream
1 bunch of radishes
parsley
1 can of asparagus (optional)

1 Half-thaw the spinach and cut into slices or cubes, sauté in butter, and add flour. Stir well. Dilute with stock, a little at a time.
2 Leave soup to simmer for a few minutes and season to taste with salt and freshly grated nutmeg.
3 Mix egg yolks and cream together, add a little soup, then pour carefully into the soup, and whisk well. The soup must not boil after you have added the egg yolks.
Serve with sliced radishes, asparagus and a sprinkling of parsley.

Brussels Sprout Soup
(serves 4)
Preparation time: about 25 min
Cooking time: about 45 min in all

4 chicken drumsticks
50g (2oz) butter
1½ litres (2½pt) chicken stock
450g (1lb) Brussels sprouts (as small as possible)
4 carrots, 1 onion
3 leeks
½–1 × 5ml tsp (½–1tsp) dried thyme
salt, dill
1 clove of garlic

1 Slice carrots and onion. Brown chicken drumsticks in ½ the butter in a large saucepan, and then add the carrots, onion and stock. Bring to the boil.
2 Slice leeks into thin rings and add to the saucepan. Simmer for about 35 min.
3 Meanwhile parboil the small sprouts. Bring lightly salted water to the boil and add the sprouts. Bring back to the boil, and then strain off the water. Cut larger sprouts in half. Add remaining butter to pan and sauté sprouts until tender.
4 Crush garlic and add this and the sprouts to the saucepan containing the soup. Simmer together for a few moments before serving, sprinkled with finely chopped dill.

Cabbage Soup (above)
(serves 4–6)
Cabbage holds in its leaves a mine of minerals which are good for us. To taste cabbage at its best, whether in a soup or as an accompanying vege-

table, cook it for as little time as possible – until *al dente*, like pasta.
Preparation time: 15 min
Cooking time: 2¼ hr in all

4–6 large potatoes
1 small celeriac or 4 stalks of celery
4–6 carrots
250g (9oz) green cabbage
2–3 × 15ml tbsp (2–3tbsp) plain
flour
For the broth: about 1.1kg (2½lb)
beef bones (with meat still on,
preferably)
salt, water

1 Barely cover bones with water and bring to the boil. Remove any scum. Add salt and leave bones to simmer for about 1½ hr (to let the meat become tender). Strain broth, and take meat off bones. Keep meat warm.
2 Add all the sliced vegetables to the stock – except for the cabbage – and boil for a further 30 min until everything is tender.
3 Mix together the plain flour and about 100ml (4fl oz) water and season to taste with salt. Add to the soup with the coarsely chopped green cabbage and leave to boil until the cabbage is just ready, still crisp. Serve soup with the reserved meat, bread and mustard.

Celery Soup
(serves 6)
Preparation time: about 15 min
Cooking time: about 20 min
Suitable for the freezer before egg yolks are added

1 head of celery
3–4 shallots or small onions
40g (1½oz) butter
1 litre (1¾pt) stock
1 × 15ml tbsp (1tbsp) plain flour
250ml (9fl oz) cream, 2 egg yolks
cress, salt, pepper
grated cheese

1 Sauté chopped shallots (or onions) and washed, finely chopped celery in 25g (1oz) of the butter on low heat. Add stock and leave to boil for about 15 min with the lid on.
2 Make little thickening beurre manié balls with remaining butter, and the plain flour. Whisk these gradually into the soup. Mix cream and egg yolks with some of the hot soup, pour back into pan, and keep the soup simmering just under boiling point. Season to taste with salt, pepper, cress and a dash of grated cheese. Serve soup hot with bread and some of the grated cheese.

Surprise Spring Soup (above)
(serves 4)
The fine, green leaves of radishes are as flavourful as the radishes themselves, so don't throw them away. Use them, with other vegetables, in this unusual soup.
In this soup we have used the leaves from two bunches of radishes. Save the radishes themselves for salads, but two could be finely chopped and added to the hot soup when serving.
Preparation time: about 15 min
Cooking time: about 25 min

2 bunches of radishes leaves (only to
be used in soup)
2 thin leeks

4 potatoes, 1 sprig of parsley
a few sprigs of fresh chervil
25g (1oz) butter
900ml (1½pt) vegetable or chicken
stock
100ml (4fl oz) single cream
salt, white pepper

1 Rinse radish leaves well and place in a saucepan with the thinly sliced leeks, peeled and sliced potatoes, ½ sprig of parsley and a little fresh chervil.
Add butter and sauté vegetables and herbs for about 5 min on a low heat.
2 Add stock, cover pan and leave soup to simmer for 15–20 min. Purée vegetables in a liquidizer or rub them through a sieve. Pour back into soup, heat and stir in cream. Season to taste.
Finely chop the rest of the parsley and chervil, and sprinkle on top of soup when serving, with toasted bread 'soldiers' or an interestingly textured brown or rye bread.

31

Golden Soups

Few will be able to resist these wonderful golden soups. As with all food, the better it looks, the better it tastes!

Sweetcorn Soup
(serves 4–6)
Preparation time: about 10 min
Cooking time: about 20 min in all

50g (2oz) butter
1 × 15ml tbsp (1tbsp) finely chopped
  onion
5 × 15ml tbsp (5tbsp) plain flour
1 × 5ml tsp (1tsp) curry powder
1 × 15ml tbsp (1tbsp) tomato purée
600ml (1pt) stock
300ml (½pt) milk
1 can sweetcorn (about 350g or ¾lb)
2–3 skinned, ripe tomatoes (or
  canned)
salt, pepper
1 green or red pepper

1 Sauté the onion in melted butter for 2–3 min on low heat. Stir in flour, curry powder and tomato purée, and slowly add the stock. Stir until the soup starts to boil, then leave to simmer for about 10 min.
2 Add milk, mashed sweetcorn and finely chopped tomatoes. Season to taste and simmer for 5 min.
3 Boil cleaned, chopped pepper in water for 5 min. Peel off the skin, mash the pepper flesh, and add to soup.

Golden Carrot Soup
(serves 4–6)
Preparation time: about 20 min
Cooking time: 30–40 min

450g (1lb) carrots
2 stalks of celery
1 onion, 25g (1oz) butter
1 × 15ml tbsp (1tbsp) oil
1 litre (1¾pt) stock
1 bay leaf
juice of ½ orange
1 × 15ml tbsp (1tbsp) lemon juice

salt, pepper
150ml (¼pt) single cream
finely chopped chives

1 Wash and peel vegetables, chop roughly, and sauté in butter and oil for 5–10 min, stirring continuously.
2 Add stock, bay leaf, orange and lemon juice, and seasonings. Leave to simmer for 25–30 min.
3 Remove bay leaf, take vegetables out of saucepan and push them through a sieve or purée in a liquidizer. Put vegetable purée back into soup saucepan. Add cream, season to taste with salt and pepper, and heat soup until near boiling.
Sprinkle with chives just before serving.

Mushroom and Cauliflower Soup (right)
(serves 6)
Preparation time: about 25 min
Cooking time: about 30 min
Suitable for the freezer, but the flavour will deteriorate

250g (9oz) mushrooms (see below)
1 onion, 250g (9oz) cauliflower
25g (1oz) butter
1 × 15ml tbsp (1tbsp) plain flour
1 litre (1¾pt) chicken stock
salt, pepper
300ml (½pt) milk, parsley

1 Finely chop the onion and sauté together with the sliced mushrooms in the butter. Add flour, stir well, and then add stock. Bring to the boil, stirring continuously.

2 Divide the cauliflower into florets and add to the saucepan. Cook for about 25–30 min.

3 Push the soup through a sieve or purée in a liquidizer. Put back into the saucepan together with the milk. Season to taste, and allow soup to simmer for a couple of minutes. Sprinkle finely chopped parsley on the soup and serve with slices of toast and ham.

NOTE If you can get hold of the yellow field chantarelles, they give the soup a nice golden colour and a delicious flavour. If you use button or cup mushrooms, add ½–1 × ml tsp (½–1tsp) turmeric to obtain the golden colour. Do not use flat mushrooms which will make the soup too dark.

Cheese Soup (left)
(serves 4–6)
Preparation time: about 25 min
Cooking time: about 30 min
Unsuitable for the freezer

40g (1½oz) butter, 2 onions
1 carrot, 1 stalk of celery
40g (1½oz) plain flour
1 litre (1¾pt) stock
salt, pepper, paprika
150g (5oz) grated Cheddar cheese

1 Sauté peeled, finely chopped or grated vegetables in butter until light gold.

2 Stir in flour and then gradually add stock. Bring to the boil, stirring, and season soup to taste with salt, pepper and paprika. Simmer for about 20 min.

3 Remove vegetables and mash them. Pour back into saucepan and heat soup until near boiling.

4 Remove saucepan from heat and stir in grated cheese, which will melt in the hot soup.

Sprinkle with crisp croûtons (see pages 24–5) just before serving.

Pumpkin Soup
(serves 6)
Preparation time: about 25 min
Cooking time: about 1 hr 10 min
Unsuitable for the freezer

1½kg (about 3¼lb) pumpkin, 1 onion
50g (2oz) butter
600ml (1pt) chicken stock
600ml (1pt) milk, salt, pepper
a pinch of nutmeg
50ml (2fl oz) double cream
finely chopped parsley

1 Peel and chop the onion. Remove the skin of the pumpkin and chop the flesh up. Sauté onion and pumpkin in butter for about 5 min until tender, but do not allow to go brown.

2 Add stock and bring to the boil. Allow the soup to simmer, covered, for about 1 hr. Push soup through a sieve or purée in a liquidizer, and replace in the pan.

3 Add milk and bring to the boil, stirring continuously. Leave to simmer for about 5 min and season to taste with salt, pepper and grated nutmeg. Finally whip in the cream and sprinkle with parsley just before serving.

Fish Soups

Fish soups feature in the cuisines of many maritime countries. On the following pages you will find many varying recipes for delicious and economical soups – although some will have to be for special occasions only! Below is a good basic recipe.

Basic Fish Soup
(serves 4–5)
Preparation time: about 25 min
Cooking time: 35 min in all
Suitable for the freezer without the mussels

700–900g (1½–2lb) fish (a mixture is best)
1 litre (1¾pt) water
1 × 5ml tsp (1tsp) salt
4 onions
1–2 cloves of garlic
4 tomatoes, 2 green peppers
1 carrot, 1 leek
½ celeriac or 4 stalks of celery
100ml (4fl oz) oil
200g (7oz) fresh steamed, or canned mussels (optional)
a pinch of saffron or turmeric
salt and white pepper

1 Wash the fish well, then bone, skin and fillet. Slice fish meat into small pieces. Place all the bones, skin, and trimmings in a saucepan, add the water and salt, bring to the boil then simmer stock for about 20 min. Strain, and retain the stock.
2 Meanwhile peel and finely chop the onions and crush the garlic. Scald, peel and quarter tomatoes. Slice cleaned peppers and leek into thin strips or rings, coarsely grate the celeriac or finely chop the celery stalks, and slice carrots thinly.
3 Heat oil in a large casserole and sauté the fish and all the vegetables for a couple of minutes. Add strained fish stock, barely covering fish and vegetables. Put the lid on and leave soup to simmer on medium heat for about 10 min.
4 Add well strained, shelled mussels (if using), mix saffron or turmeric with some of the boiling stock and add to the soup. Leave to simmer for a further 5 min and season soup to taste with salt and pepper.
Serve with chunks of crisp French bread.

Basic Fish Soup
1 Wash the fish, and cut off the tail and fins. Remove skin if you want, and slice fish into pieces.

2 Heat oil in a large casserole, and sauté fish and the sliced, cleaned vegetables for a couple of minutes on strong heat.

3 Add enough strained fish stock to just cover the contents of the casserole.

4 Freshly steamed and shelled or canned mussels are added to the soup at the last minute, along with the saffron or turmeric.

Above: Cod and Shrimp Soup.

Cod and Shrimp Soup

(serves 4)
Preparation time: 20–30 min
Cooking time: 25 min
Unsuitable for the freezer

450g (1lb) shrimps
25g (1oz) butter
450g (1lb) cod fillet
1 litre (1¾pt) water
1 onion, salt, pepper
1 crustless slice of white bread
1 × 5ml tsp (1tsp) grated lemon rind
1 × 5ml tsp (1tsp) chives or thyme
150ml (¼pt) double cream
1 egg yolk
juice of ½ lemon
a pinch of nutmeg

1 Sauté pieces of fish and shrimp shells in butter together with finely chopped onion, chives and lemon rind. Pour 1 litre (1¾pt) water over, bring to the boil and simmer for 20 min. Strain stock. Discard shrimp shells, and keep pieces of cod.

2 Soak slice of white bread in stock and crumble thoroughly. Finely chop half the shrimps and put in a saucepan with butter, lemon juice and nutmeg. Add stock, stirring, and leave to simmer for about 5 min. Push through a sieve or purée in a liquidizer.

3 Whisk egg yolk and cream together and add a little hot soup. Pour mixture back into the soup pan. Stir in the remaining shrimps and cod, and heat everything thoroughly (do *not* allow to boil). Garnish with dill and season soup to taste with salt and pepper.

This cod and shrimp soup is very filling, and if served as a first course it will feed 6–8. Accompany with crisp French bread and butter.

Simple Shrimp Soup

You can buy shrimp soup in cans, and serve it as it is, but it will be even tastier if you add that little extra something.

Heat soup and season to taste with a little dry sherry or vermouth. Some cream will give it a full, rich taste, and a few peeled shrimps will finish it off. Serve with sour cream and crisp French bread.

How to Peel Shrimps

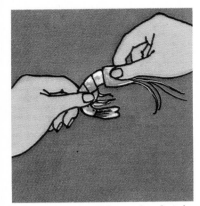

1 Holding the tail in one hand, twist off the head with the other.

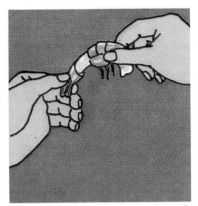

2 Hold the shelled body and gently pull off tail.

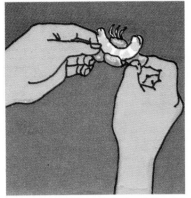

3 Peel away the soft body shell, with the legs, and roe if any.

Shellfish Soup

(serves 4)
Preparation time: about 15 min
Cooking time: 4–5 min
Unsuitable for the freezer

about 40 freshly steamed mussels (or the same quantity of canned)
3–4 lobster claws or 6 scallops, (sautéed in a little butter)
2 × 15ml tbsp (2tbsp) oil, 1 onion
2 × 5ml tsp (2tsp) curry powder
2 cloves of garlic, 2 tomatoes
400ml ($\frac{3}{4}$pt) mussel or fish stock
100ml (4fl oz) dry white wine
juice of $\frac{1}{2}$ lemon
100ml (4fl oz) double cream
1 egg yolk
15g ($\frac{1}{2}$oz) butter, salt
parsley

1 Finely chop the onion and saute with the crushed garlic and curry powder in oil for a couple of minutes. Scald and peel the tomatoes, slice them finely and place in pan. Add stock and white wine and bring to the boil.

2 Place steamed mussels and sliced lobster meat or sautéed scallops in pan and allow soup to simmer for about 4 min. Remove from heat. Mix together egg yolk and cream with some of the hot soup and pour back into pan. Stir in butter to make the soup shiny and serve with chopped parsley.

Shellfish Soup. A really luxurious soup made with lobster or scallops and mussels.

Left: Green Pea Soup and butter-fried curried shrimps, an unusual – and delicious – combination.

stock, and leave to simmer for 5–10 min. Season to taste with salt, pepper, paprika and Madeira or sherry.

3 Whisk egg yolk and mix with whipped cream. Add some of the hot soup to the egg, and stir the mixture carefully back into the soup. Add crab meat and heat, but do not allow to boil.

This recipe can also be made with lobster, for a really luxurious soup. Use some white wine instead of some of the fish stock.

Cod and Shellfish Soup

(serves 4)
Preparation time: about 10 min
Cooking time: about 25 min in all
Unsuitable for the freezer

15g (½oz) butter
1 × 15ml tbsp (1tbsp) olive oil
a pinch of saffron or turmeric
1 onion, 1 clove of garlic
1 bulb fennel or 3–4 stalks of celery
salt, pepper
about 700ml (1¼pt) fish stock
½ can tomatoes
200ml (7fl oz) dry white wine
about 450g (1lb) cod fillets
1 can of mussels
50–100g (2–4oz) shrimps
fresh dill and parsley

1 Sauté saffron or turmeric in oil and butter and add finely chopped onion and crushed garlic. Slice the fennel or celery finely, add to the pan, and leave everything to sauté for about 5 min. Add salt and pepper, fish stock, tomatoes and white wine.

2 Allow soup to simmer for about 5 min and add cod, sliced into small pieces. Allow soup to simmer on low heat until the fish is white and firm. Add mussels, shrimps, finely chopped parsley and dill. Heat soup until nearly boiling and serve immediately.

Green Pea Soup with Curried Shrimps and Rice

Prepare Green Pea Soup, following the recipe on page 20, but add a dash of fish stock to give it a thinner consistency.

Serve with rice and curried shrimps.

Curried Shrimps

Melt 40–50g (1½–2oz) butter or 3–4 × 15ml tbsp (3–4tbsp) oil in a saucepan and add 1–2 × 5ml tsp (1–2tsp) strong curry powder, 1 × 5ml tsp (1tsp) paprika, and 2 crushed cloves of garlic. Leave to sauté for a couple of minutes and add peeled shrimps. Stir-fry quickly on strong heat until they change colour. Do not allow the curry sauce to burn.

Crab Soup

(serves 4)
Preparation time: 15–20 min
Cooking time: 5–10 min
Unsuitable for the freezer

Meat from 1 crab or 2 cans
25g (1oz) butter
2 × 15ml tbsp (2tbsp) plain flour
1 litre (1¾pt) fish stock
salt, pepper
paprika
2–3 × 15ml tbsp (2–3tbsp) dry
*   Madeira or sherry*
1 egg yolk
100ml (4fl oz) double cream

1 Take all the meat out of the crab shells and cut very small.

2 Melt butter, stir in flour and

One crab makes a delicious Crab Soup to serve four.

Creole Fish Soup

(serves 4)
Preparation time: about 20 min
Cooking time: about 25 min

900g (2lb) fish (cod, halibut etc)
1 onion
25–40g (1–1½oz) butter or
  2–3 × 15ml tbsp (2–3tbsp) oil
1 × 15ml tbsp (1tbsp) plain flour
1 can tomatoes
1 clove of garlic (optional)
2 bay leaves, paprika
juice of ½ lemon
parsley, marjoram, mixed spice
150ml (¼pt) red wine (optional)

1 litre (1¾pt) fish stock
salt, cayenne pepper

1 Fry finely chopped onion in butter or oil until golden. Stir in flour and add the chopped tomatoes and crushed garlic. Stir in wine, lemon juice, tomato juice from can, and enough fish stock to give the right consistency. Add spices, finely chopped herbs and salt to taste. Leave soup to boil for 5–10 min.
2 Clean and slice fish fillets. Leave in the simmering soup until ready. Serve soup piping hot, with potatoes or small slices of bread.

This fish soup, made from the basic recipe, but with delicious additions, is garnished with black olives just before serving.

Russian Salmon Soup

(serves 4)
Preparation time: about 20 min
Cooking time: 45 min in all
Unsuitable for the freezer

about 450g (1lb) fresh salmon
2 litres (3½pt) water
bouquet garni of parsley and green

part of leeks
2 onions, 2 leeks, 1 carrot
¼ celeriac or 2 stalks celery
50g (2oz) butter
1 bay leaf
2–3 cloves of garlic
1–2 sprigs of thyme
5–6 peppercorns
2–3 × 15ml tbsp (2–3tbsp) tomato
   purée
50g (2oz) green olives
1–2 × 15ml tbsp (1–2tbsp) capers
salt
3–4 × 15ml tbsp (3–4tbsp) sour
   cream

1 Clean the fish, skin and bone, and simmer the skin and bones with the bouquet garni and water to make a stock (about 25 min). Strain.

2 Peel onions, leeks, carrot and celeriac or celery, and slice finely. Sauté for a few minutes in butter without browning. Add strained fish stock, tomato purée and coarsely chopped olives. Put the bay leaf, garlic, thyme and peppercorns in a small muslin bag and add to the soup pan. Simmer for about 15 min.

3 Cube salmon meat and add to the soup. Leave soup to simmer on low heat for about 10 min. Add capers. Taste the soup and season further with salt or add a chicken stock cube if the flavour is a bit weak.

Stir in sour cream, or you can serve the sour cream separately, in dollops on top of the soup.

Serve with bread.

Belgian Fish Soup or Waterzooi

(serves 4–5)

The Belgians are famous for their good food and one of their specialities is *Waterzooi*, which is eaten like a soup, but is more like a stew.

Preparation time: 15–20 min
Cooking time: about 20 min
Unsuitable for the freezer

2kg (about 4¼lb) fish (eel, cod,
   halibut etc)
200g (7oz) celeriac
salt, pepper
water + white wine
100g (4oz) butter
2 × 15ml tbsp (2tbsp) breadcrumbs
bouquet garni of parsley, thyme and
   bay leaf

1 Finely chop or grate peeled celeriac. Clean, bone and skin the fish and slice the fillets. Place celeriac at the bottom of a saucepan or flame-proof casserole and place fish slices on top. Sprinkle with salt and pepper and add bouquet garni. Add water and white wine until the fish is covered (twice as much water as wine). Place the butter in dollops on top and poach fish on low heat until firm.

2 Remove fish slices and place them in hot individual soup dishes or in a deep serving dish. Strain stock and stir in breadcrumbs. Bring the stock to the boil once again and pour over fish.

Serve with white bread spread with cooled celeriac from the stock, mashed with a little butter, salt and pepper.

Party Fish Soup

This fish soup is made from the basic recipe on page 34, but with a few extras. Add 200ml (7fl oz) white wine to the fish stock, the juice of 1 lemon, and ½–1 × ml tsp (½–1tsp) dried thyme. Mussels, shrimps, crawfish tails or any other fresh or canned shellfish can be added to suit your taste, your pocket and the occasion.

Finally thicken the soup with 2 egg yolks mixed with a little warm stock.

A bowlful of hot, aromatic fish soup makes a filling and tasty start to a dinner party.

Mussel Soup with Sour Cream is a tasty first course.

Mussel Soup with Sour Cream

(serves 6)
Preparation time: 10–15 min
Cooking time: 10 min
Unsuitable for the freezer

30–40 fresh steamed mussels or the equivalent amount of canned
1 leek
150–250g (5–9oz) mushrooms
40–50g (1½–2oz) butter
2–3 × 15ml tbsp (2–3tbsp) flour
1.2 litres (about 2pt) stock (mussel, other fish or vegetable stock)
100ml (4fl oz) single cream
100ml (4fl oz) sour cream
salt, white pepper
saffron or turmeric

1 Clean and slice mushrooms. Wash the leek and slice into rings. Sauté vegetables in about half the butter for a few minutes on low heat.
2 Remove mushrooms and leek. Add more butter to the pan and stir in flour. Add the stock gradually, stirring, and leave to simmer for about 10 min on low heat. Strain soup if necessary.
3 Whisk together cream and sour cream, add some of the hot stock and pour mixture carefully back into casserole. Add mushrooms, leek and shelled mussels and heat soup thoroughly, but do not boil. If you wish to add a bit of colour to the soup, stir a pinch of saffron or turmeric in water or stock and add as a final touch.

Tomato Soup with Mussels and Rice

(serves 4)
Preparation time: about 10 min
Cooking time: 15 min
Unsuitable for the freezer

50ml (2fl oz) olive oil, 1 large onion
1–2 cloves of garlic
1 can of tomatoes
1 × 5ml tsp (1tsp) dried basil
salt, pepper
1 litre (1¾pt) chicken stock (or water + cube)
50g (2oz) boiled, long-grain rice
1 can of mussels

1 Peel and chop the onion, crush the garlic and sauté both in oil until onion is shiny. Add chopped to-matoes, with their juice, basil, salt and pepper.
2 Leave mixture to simmer for 3–4 min, then add stock, and simmer for about 10 min more.
3 Add cooked rice and drained mussels, and allow to heat through. Season to taste.
You can also use canned tomato soup for this recipe. Season to taste with spices and add rice and mussels.
Serve with brown bread, grated cheese or slices of cheese, or you can make some little hot cheese toasts. Spread a thin layer of butter on slices of brown bread. Place plenty of grated cheese on top and bake in a hot oven (or grill) until the cheese melts and turns golden.

Fish Balls or Quenelles

Small, homemade fish balls are both tasty and look nice in fish soup. Mince 450g (1lb) cod fillet together with 2 egg yolks and 100g (4oz) soft butter, and then push through a fine-mesh sieve. Chill. Beat when chilled, and add salt, pepper and nutmeg. Gradually beat in 2 egg whites, and about 200ml (7fl oz) double cream, until you have a creamy, light, consistency. Chill well before shaping into balls. Bring some chicken or fish stock, or plain water, to the boil in a shallow sauce-pan. Shape the quenelles between 2 small spoons and drop into the boil-ing stock. When the pan is full, lower the heat, cover, and poach for about 10–15 min.

Tomato Soup with Mussels and Rice. Use canned tomatoes to save time.

Old-fashioned Fish Soups

In Norway and Sweden, hearty fish soups are tradition fare. Take a tip from the Scandinavians and serve these dishes to keep out the cold.

Fish Soup with Haddock Balls

Make fish soup from haddock, following the basic recipe on page 34. To give the soup a richer flavour, you can add a few shrimps, mussels or other shellfish, with plenty of finely chopped parsley or other herbs. And to make it a bit more exciting, you can add haddock balls at the last minute.

Haddock Balls

To get a reasonable consistency, as in this recipe, put the fish through the mincer twice, but if you want your haddock balls finer, you can mince the fish several times.

250g (9oz) fresh haddock fillet
50g (2oz) fresh belly of pork
1 × 15ml tbsp (1tbsp) cornflour
$\frac{1}{2}$ × 5ml tsp ($\frac{1}{2}$tsp) salt, pepper
100ml (4fl oz) milk

1 Slice haddock, and mince twice (or more) with the chopped belly of pork.
2 Stir in seasonings and cornflour and dilute with the milk, a little at a time.
3 Shape into small oblongs or balls and poach them in lightly salted boiling water for about 8 min.

Herring Soup with Barley
(serves 4)
Preparation time: about 30 min
Soaking time for barley: 10–12 hr
Cooking time: 2 hr in all
Unsuitable for the freezer

6 fresh herrings
75g (3oz) barley
1 small swede
2 potatoes
¼ celeriac or 2 stalks celery
1 small onion
1 × 15ml tbsp (1 tbsp) finely chopped
  chives
salt, pepper, thyme

1 Soak barley overnight and boil in
the soaking water for about 1½ hr in
a large saucepan.
2 Clean the herrings and poach or
steam in a little water. Keep fish
warm and retain stock.
3 Peel onion, celeriac (or trim
celery), swede and potatoes. Cut
everything into cubes. Add vegetables to the barley saucepan. Add
more liquid if necessary and simmer
until vegetables are nearly tender.
4 Strain herring stock and pour into
the soup, with the pieces of fish. Add
thyme and chives and season with
salt and pepper.
A herring soup should have a strong,
fresh flavour. Serve with boiled potatoes and butter or sour cream.

Mackerel Soup
(serves 4)
Preparation time: about 20 min
Cooking time: 5–10 min
Unsuitable for the freezer

450–700g (1–1½lb) mackerel
1 chicken stock cube
6 white peppercorns
1 × 5ml tbsp (1 tbsp) salt, 1 bay leaf
4–5 whole allspice berries
4 small potatoes, 1 leek
1–2 red peppers
finely chopped dill

1 Bring 1 litre (1¾pt) water to the
boil with salt, peppercorns, allspice
berries, bay leaf and stock cube. (Or
use 1 litre (1¾pt) fish stock if you
have any.)
2 Add peeled potato, cut into cubes,
and boil until almost tender.
3 Clean the fish and slice. Clean leek
and peppers and slice in strips.
4 Place the fish slices and the vegetables in the saucepan and allow
soup to simmer gently until fish and
vegetables are ready. Serve with lots
of finely chopped dill and slices of
bread and butter.

*Left: Fish Soup with Haddock Balls
and added shellfish.*

Old-fashioned Herring Soup
(serves 6–8)
Preparation time: about 30 min
Cooking time: about 20 min

1½kg (about 3¼lb) small fresh
  herrings
1 onion
450g (1lb) potatoes
6 black peppercorns
1 slice of brown bread with butter
1 × 15ml tbsp (1 tbsp) finely chopped
  parsley

1 Peel the potatoes and cut in four.
Boil in lightly salted water for about
10 min (until par-cooked).
2 Clean the herrings and place in
the saucepan with the potatoes along
with finely chopped onion, brown
bread and herbs and spices.
3 Leave soup to simmer, covered,
on low heat until the herrings and
the potatoes are ready. Remove
bread and serve soup hot with bread
and butter.

Bergen Fish Soup
(serves 4)
Preparation time: 10–15 min
Cooking time: 40 min

about 1kg (2¼lb) fresh haddock
2 litres (3½pt) water
2 × 5ml tsp (2tsp) salt
3–4 black peppercorns
1 bay leaf, 2–3 carrots
1 parsnip
1 × 15ml tbsp (1 tbsp) plain flour
100ml (4fl oz) sour cream
1 × 5ml tsp (1 tsp) sugar
1 bunch of chives

1 Clean the fish and slice into small
bits. Place in a large saucepan, add
water and remove any scum.
2 Add bay leaf, salt and peppercorns and leave to simmer for about
30 min, without covering, until the
liquid has reduced by ¼. Strain stock
and keep fish warm.
3 Put stock back in saucepan, and
add cleaned, sliced vegetables.
Leave to simmer until nearly tender.
Add thickening of plain flour mixed
with some of the stock and leave
soup to simmer for a further 5 min.
4 Mix sour cream and sugar in a
deep serving soup dish, add the fish
meat, and pour soup over. Sprinkle
with finely chopped chives.
Serve soup hot with a few tasty fish
balls and boiled potatoes or bread.

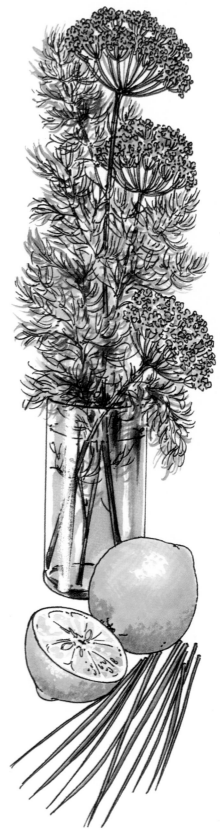

One Course Soups

These filling and thick soups are good, warming autumn and winter fare.

Chicken Soup with Vegetables

(serves 4)
Preparation time: 15–20 min
Cooking time: about 1 hr, 25 min in all
Unsuitable for the freezer

1 large chicken or boiling fowl
1 small cauliflower
2–3 stalks of celery
1 leek, 2 carrots, 1 onion
1 small packet of frozen peas
2 × 15ml tbsp (2tbsp) oil
salt, white pepper
about 100g (4oz) spaghetti

1 Boil chicken in lightly salted water until meat is tender and comes away from the bones (about 45–60 min). Retain the liquid.
2 Boil spaghetti until *al dente*.
3 Slice scraped and peeled vegetables, and sauté in a large saucepan in the oil for 5 min (*not* the peas).
4 Pour 1 litre (1¾pt) chicken broth over vegetables and leave to boil on low heat until tender. Add frozen peas, sliced chicken meat and cooked spaghetti. Season soup to taste with salt and pepper and serve piping hot with bread.

Lamb and Bean Soup

(serves 4)
Preparation time: about 15 min
Cooking time: 1 hr, 15 min in all
Suitable for the freezer

600g (1lb 5oz) lean lamb or mutton
1kg (about 2¼lb) fresh, canned or
  frozen green beans
2 × 15ml tbsp (2tbsp) oil, 2 onions
salt, black pepper
1 litre (1¾pt) meat or vegetable stock
¼ × 5ml tsp (¼tsp) rosemary
1 × 5ml tsp (1tsp) marjoram

Three warming and filling soups, from top, clockwise: Fish Soup made from basic recipe on page 34, replacing mussels with shrimps and adding a couple of extra carrots; Chicken Soup with Vegetables and spaghetti; and Lamb and Bean Soup.

47

Right: Pork and Brussels Sprout
Soup.
Left: Cabbage Soup with Pork.

*1.4 litres (2½pt) meat or vegetable
stock*
*450g (1lb) lean pork (shoulder or
hand and spring)*
450g (1lb) potatoes, 1–2 carrots
300g (11oz) Brussels sprouts
salt, pepper
marjoram and/or thyme

1 Cut skin and fat off pork, and
place in boiling stock. Bring back to
the boil, skim well, and leave to
simmer, covered, for 1 hr.
2 Meanwhile peel potatoes and carrots, and cube. Remove meat from
stock and cut into cubes. Put everything back into the saucepan and
boil for a further 30 min.
3 Clean the sprouts (halved if they
are large) and add to pan for the last
10 min. Season to taste with salt,
pepper and finely chopped herbs.
Serve with bread or rolls.

Cabbage Soup with Pork
(serves 4)
Preparation time: 15–20 min
Soaking time: 10–12 hr
Cooking time: 1¼ hr in all
Unsuitable for the freezer

450g (1lb) belly of pork
1 medium cabbage
225g (½lb) haricot beans
3–4 potatoes, 2 carrots
1 leek, 2 onions
1 turnip or piece of swede
1 clove of garlic (optional)
thyme, salt, pepper

1 Soak the beans in water for about
10–12 hr, and then drain.
2 Parboil the cabbage in boiling
water for a couple of minutes and
slice. Clean vegetables and peel or
scrape, and then place soaked beans,
sliced cabbage, large potato cubes,
chopped onions, sliced turnip and
carrot, leek rings and crushed garlic
in a saucepan. Add water to cover.
Add salt and pepper and leave vegetables to simmer for about 15 min.
3 Slice belly of pork, or cut into
cubes, and put in saucepan. Cook
for a further 1 hr.
Serve with fried bread. Fry 1 slice of
bread per person in butter until
golden.

1 Cube the meat and brown lightly
in oil in a large pan. Add chopped
onions and sauté with the meat.
2 Add boiling stock and leave
everything to simmer, covered, for
about 1 hr.
3 Wash and clean fresh beans. Slice
them in two or four, add to saucepan
with meat and boil for 15 min until
meat and beans are tender. Frozen
beans should be cooked for 10 min,
and canned beans should only be
heated for a few minutes.
Season with salt, pepper and herbs.

Vegetable Soup with Pork
(serves 4)
Preparation time: about 20 min
Cooking time: about 15 min
Suitable for the freezer

125g (4½oz) lean belly of pork
25g (1oz) butter
2 × 15ml tbsp (2tbsp) oil
2 onions, 2 cloves of garlic
1 × 5ml tsp (1tsp) dried basil
1 × 5ml tsp (1tsp) dried chervil

salt, white pepper
300–400g (11–14oz) white cabbage
2–3 carrots, 2 leeks
1.4 litres (2½pt) stock
1 small packet of frozen peas
1 sprig of parsley, finely chopped

1 Cut pork into cubes. Fry in butter
and oil in a large pan, and add chopped onions, crushed garlic and herbs
and seasonings.
2 Wash and shred or slice the cabbage, carrots and leeks, place in
saucepan and sauté for a couple of
minutes.
3 Add stock and leave soup to
simmer on low heat until vegetables
are tender. Add peas and sprinkle
with a generous amount of chopped
parsley.
Serve soup with brown bread.

Pork and Brussels Sprout Soup
(serves 4)
Preparation time: about 20 min
Cooking time: 1½ hr in all
Suitable for the freezer

International Soups

Just about every country has its own soup speciality, and on the following pages, we give our recipes for some well-known and less well-known soups from far and near.

Italian Minestrone
(serves 4)
Preparation time: 15 min
Cooking time: about 15 min

There are nearly as many variations of this vegetable soup, as there are housewives in Italy! In this one we have used both white beans and pasta, to make the soup filling and capable of being served as a meal on its own.

1 large can of tomatoes
1 litre (1¾pt) stock
1–2 × 15ml tbsp (1–2tbsp) olive oil
2 small carrots
1 aubergine
1–2 courgettes
1 can of white beans
1 packet of frozen peas (about 200g or 7oz)
100g (4oz) cooked pasta (short macaroni, shells, farfalli etc)
salt, pepper, basil

Above: Delicious Minestrone from Italy.

1 Coarsely chop the canned tomatoes and place in a saucepan with their juice. Add stock and oil and bring to the boil.
2 Scrape and slice carrots and cut aubergine and courgettes into cubes. Place vegetables in saucepan and leave soup to simmer for about 10 min or until the vegetables are nearly tender.
3 Add drained beans, frozen peas and cooked pasta and re-heat the soup. Season to taste with salt, pepper and finely crushed basil.
Serve piping hot with bread and grated Parmesan cheese.

Belgian Oxtail Soup

(serves 4–6)
Preparation time: about 30 min
Cooking time: about 2 hr

1 oxtail, 2 litres (3½pt) stock
salt, pepper, flour
butter, oil
2–3 carrots
2–3 onions
4–6 stalks of celery
2 cloves of garlic
Bouquet garni of celery leaves, 4–5
 parsley stalks, and 2 bay leaves

1 Trim as much fat as possible from the jointed oxtail, and turn joints in flour mixed with salt and pepper. Fry them in a mixture of butter and oil on a low heat in a large pan. Add boiling stock, crushed garlic and bouquet garni. Leave to simmer on low heat for about 2 hr, covered.
2 Meanwhile wash and peel the vegetables and slice. Sauté for a few minutes on low heat in butter and oil, but do not allow to go brown.
3 Just before the meat is ready, add the vegetables. Leave soup to simmer until vegetables are tender. Remove meat and vegetables and keep warm. Remove bouquet garni, and strain the stock.
4 Melt 15g (½oz) butter in a saucepan, mix in 1 × 15ml tbsp (1tbsp) plain flour, and leave to sauté on low heat until lightly golden. Add hot stock gradually and stir vigorously to make it shiny and smooth. Mix in stock until the soup has the right consistency and then put meat and vegetables back into saucepan. Serve with bread and some grated Parmesan cheese.

Swedish Bean Soup

(serves 4)
Preparation time: 5 min
Soaking time: about 12 hr
Cooking time: 4–6 hr
Oven temperature: about 200°C, 400°F, Gas 6

300g (11oz) red kidney beans
200g (7oz) lightly salted pork
3 litres (about 5pt) stock
salt, sugar, vinegar

1 Soak beans overnight.
2 Pour off soaking water and place beans and cubed pork in a casserole or ovenproof dish. Sprinkle with a little sugar, salt and 1 × 15ml tbsp

(1tbsp) vinegar. Pour stock on top of beans and pork. Cover with a tight-fitting lid or doubled tin foil.
3 Leave casserole in the bottom of the oven for at least 4, preferably 6, hours. Check from time to time. If too much liquid has evaporated, add more stock.

Dutch Pork Soup

(serves 4)
Preparation time: 10–15 min
Cooking time: 1½ hr in all

1kg (about 2¼lb) lightly salted pork
about 1½ litres (2½pt) water
450g (1lb) white cabbage
450g (1lb) carrots
450g (1lb) potatoes
finely chopped parsley

Above : Oxtail makes a filling, brown soup, which features in many national cuisines.

1 Boil pork in water for about 1 hr. Remove from pan and slice. Strain stock.
2 While the pork is cooking, shred the cabbage, and slice carrots and potatoes.
3 Add vegetables and pork to the pork stock and simmer for a further 30 min on low heat.
Sprinkle with finely chopped parsley and serve soup with slices of bread.

Economical Soups

Celery or Celeriac Soup with Rice

(serves 4)
Preparation time: about 10 min
Cooking time: about 25 min in all
Suitable for the freezer

1 large celeriac or 1 head of celery
100g (4oz) belly of pork
40g (1½oz) rice, 1 onion
25g (1oz) butter
1¼ litres (2pt) stock
salt, pepper

1 Slice pork into thin strips and brown lightly with the finely chopped onion in butter.
2 Coarsely grate, or slice celery finely and add to the saucepan with the rice. Leave to sauté for a couple of minutes with the pork and onion. Add the stock. Season to taste, and simmer for about 10 min.

Consommé with Meatballs

(serves 4)
Preparation time: about 25 min
Cooking time: about 15 min
Consommé or stock, and meatballs, can be frozen separately

1.4 litres (2½pt) good meat stock
  (see page 5)
1–2 × 15ml tbsp (1–2tbsp) tomato
  purée
4–5 × 15ml tbsp (4–5tbsp)
  breadcrumbs
finely chopped parsley and chervil
meatballs :
250g (9oz) minced lean lamb
250g (9oz) minced lean pork
1 clove of garlic
2–3 × 15ml tbsp (2–3tbsp)
  breadcrumbs
1 large or 2 small eggs
salt, pepper, paprika
plain flour
butter or oil

1 To make the meatballs, crush the garlic and mix with minced meats and seasonings. Stir in the egg(s) and add a few breadcrumbs if the mixture is too sloppy.
2 Shape small meatballs, roll them in flour and fry until nice and brown in butter or oil on even heat.
3 Bring good meat stock to the boil and stir in breadcrumbs. Season with tomato purée, parsley and chervil. Add meatballs and leave to simmer for about 15 min.

Potato Soup with Smoked Sausages (below)

(serves 4)
Preparation time: about 25 min
Cooking time: about 20 min
Unsuitable for the freezer

250–300g (9–11oz) potatoes
1 onion, 1 leek
40g (1½oz) butter
2 × 15ml tbsp (2tbsp) tomato purée
½ × 5ml tsp (½tsp) dried basil
2 bay leaves
1 litre (1¾pt) stock (or
  water + cube)

2–3 thin smoked sausages
100g (4oz) frozen spinach
4 tomatoes, 1 sprig of dill
salt, pepper, nutmeg
100ml (4fl oz) cream

1 Peel and scrape vegetables. Chop the onion, slice leek into rings and the potatoes into cubes.

2 Sauté in 25g (1oz) butter for a couple of minutes. Add tomato purée, basil, bay leaves and stock. Cover pan and simmer for about 20 min on low heat.

3 Slice the sausages and put into soup.

4 Defrost the spinach in a colander, roughly chop the tomatoes and finely chop the dill. Sauté together in remaining butter until everything is tender. Purée mixture in a liquidizer or press through a sieve.

5 Add spinach and tomato purée to the sausage and potato soup. Mix well and season to taste with salt, pepper and nutmeg and finally stir in cream.

Easy Vegetable Soup
(serves 4)
Preparation time: about 10 min
Cooking time: about 15 min
Suitable for the freezer

150–200g (5–7oz) bacon or belly
    pork
2 × 15ml tbsp (2tbsp) long-grain rice
1 litre (1¾pt) good stock
about 400g (14oz) frozen vegetables
    or 200g (7oz) finely chopped
    white cabbage
2–3 × 15ml tbsp (2–3tbsp) tomato
    purée
salt, pepper, marjoram
finely chopped parsley

1 Slice or cut bacon or pork into bits, and brown quickly with rice in a saucepan. Add a little butter if the meat is lean.

2 Add boiling stock, vegetables, tomato purée, salt, pepper and marjoram. Bring back to the boil and simmer on low heat until vegetables are tender (about 15 min). Season again if necessary and sprinkle with finely chopped parsley.

A rich vegetable soup is filling and can be infinitely varied, depending on the stock you use, and the choice of vegetables. Serve with bread, butter and grated cheese to sprinkle on top for a complete meal.

Vegetable soups can also be made from mixed, frozen vegetables. Here finely chopped cabbage and chunks of belly pork are the main ingredients.

53

Chicken Soups

Clear chicken broth, made from boiling a chicken, is nice by itself, but you can add vegetables or meat to it, and thicken with egg yolks, cream or cheese to get a delicious, filling dish fit for any occasion!

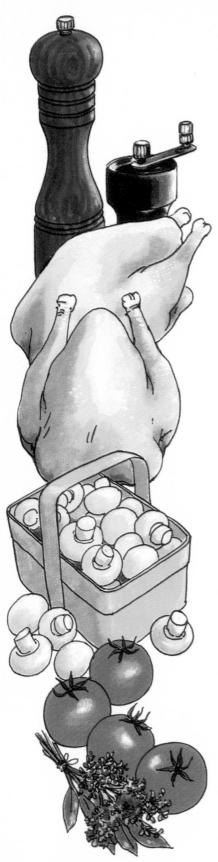

Clear Chicken Soup

(serves 5–6)
Preparation time: about 15–20 min
Cooking time: about 1½ hr
Suitable for the freezer without herbs and spices

1 large chicken or boiling fowl
about 2 litres (3½pt) chicken stock
* (or water + cube)*
4 onions
3 tomatoes
2 × 15ml tbsp (2tbsp) oil
salt, pepper
6 coriander seeds
bay leaf
finely chopped parsley and/or chervil

1 Wipe the chicken, and submerge in stock in a deep saucepan (if necessary, half the bird). Bring to the boil and remove any scum from the surface.
2 Finely chop the onions, slice tomatoes thinly, and sauté in oil for a couple of minutes or until the onions look shiny.
3 Add to the stock in the deep pan, along with the salt, pepper, coriander and bay leaf. Cover and simmer on low heat for about 1½ hr.
4 Lift the chicken from the soup; remove skin and bones from the chicken flesh, and cut flesh into small pieces. Strain stock, replace meat in stock, and sprinkle with finely chopped herbs.

Cold Curried Chicken Soup

(serves 6)
Preparation time: about 15 min
Unsuitable for the freezer

1 litre (1¾pt) chicken stock
2 × 15ml tbsp (2tbsp) finely chopped
* onions*
25g (1oz) butter
2 × 15ml tbsp (2tbsp) curry powder
1 × 15ml tbsp (1tbsp) plain flour
4 egg yolks
250ml (9fl oz) double cream
100g (4oz) cooked chicken meat

1 Sauté the onion in butter until shiny. Stir in curry powder and flour and leave to sauté on low heat for about 5 min.
2 Add boiling stock gradually and stir until the soup is smooth. Mix egg yolks with 2 × 15ml tbsp (2tbsp) hot soup, and pour back into saucepan. Allow soup to simmer on low heat for about 1 min. Do *not* boil!
3 Strain soup and add cream, stirring continuously. Place sliced chicken meat in soup. Cool the soup before serving, and place some coarsely crushed ice or a couple of ice-cubes in each soup dish.

Thickened Chicken Soup

(serves 4)
Preparation time: about 5 min
Cooking time: a few min
Unsuitable for the freezer

1 litre (1¾pt) chicken stock (from a
* boiled chicken)*
15g (½oz) butter
2 × 15ml tbsp (2tbsp) plain flour
2 egg yolks
3–4 × 15ml tbsp (3–4tbsp) grated
* cheese*
250ml (9fl oz) double cream
salt, pepper

1 Melt butter and stir in flour. Gradually add boiling stock and stir well over low heat for a few minutes.
2 Mix together cheese, egg yolks, cream and some of the stock.
3 Remove soup saucepan from the heat and whisk in the egg and cream mixture. Season soup to taste with salt and pepper, and re-heat gently. Serve with croissants, butter and cheese, or just grated cheese.

Clear Chicken Soup.

Cold Soups

Really hot days are few and far between, but when appetites are small because of heat, a good cold soup is easy to prepare and delicious to eat.

Gazpacho
(serves 4)
There are many variations of this Spanish soup, but they all have one thing in common: they are made of raw salad vegetables. The soup should be well chilled before serving.

Preparation time: about 30 min
Cooling time: 2 hr
Unsuitable for the freezer

1 clove of garlic
2 × 5ml tsp (2tsp) caraway seeds
1 × 5ml tsp (1tsp) paprika
2 tomatoes, 2 red or green peppers
1.4 litre (2½pt) water or light stock
2 × 15ml tbsp (2tbsp) olive oil
1 finely chopped onion
about ½ cucumber
1 slice of white bread
salt, 1 × 15ml tbsp (1tbsp) vinegar
ice cubes

1 Crush the garlic well with the caraway seeds and paprika (preferably in a mortar).
2 Scald, peel and chop the tomatoes. Finely chop 1 cleaned pepper and mash tomatoes and pepper together with the spice mixture,

Above: A plate of cold Gazpacho is refreshing on a hot summer's day.

then put in a large bowl.
3 Stir in about 1.4 litre (2½pt) cold water or light stock and the olive oil. Add chopped onion, the other pepper and the cucumber, cubed finely, and crustless bread which has been soaked in a little water. Season to taste with salt and vinegar. Cover bowl, and leave soup in the refrigerator for about 2 hr.
Serve soup with a couple of icecubes in each plate, accompanied by crisp French bread. You could, if you like, purée the soup ingredients for a smoother soup, with which you can serve separate little plates of cubed red and green pepper, parsley, onion, olives, croûtons etc.

Cold Tomato Soup

(serves 4)
Preparation time: about 20 min
Unsuitable for the freezer

6–8 ripe tomatoes
½ cucumber
1 red pepper, 1 onion
1 clove of garlic (optional)
salt, pepper, marjoram
a little olive oil and wine vinegar
parsley

1 Scald, peel and mash tomatoes. Slice the cucumber finely or cut into small cubes.
2 Finely chop the pepper and slice onion into paper-thin rings.
3 Mix all vegetables in a large bowl, and season to taste with salt, pepper and marjoram. Add crushed garlic (if using) and a little olive oil and wine vinegar.
4 Dilute with ice-cold water or cold chicken stock until the soup reaches the right consistency.
Serve with ice cubes and a generous amount of finely chopped parsley.

Jellied Consommé

This soup, an easy first course to serve, is based on canned consommé. When the cans are left in the refrigerator for a few hours the contents turn to jelly. Allow 150ml (¼pt) consommé per head. Place the jelly in small bowls, using a spoon. Add sour cream and 'caviar' or mushrooms.

Sour Cream and 'Caviar'

A large dollop of sour cream and 1–2 × 5ml tsp (1–2tsp) black or red lumpfish roe, with finely chopped parsley on top.

Mushrooms

Cut a few raw, cleaned, button mushrooms into thin slices, and sprinkle with lemon juice. Allow to stand for a few minutes, then place on top of the jellied consommé. Sprinkle with finely chopped parsley or chives.

Crème Vichyssoise

(serves 4)
Preparation and cooking: about 30 min + cooling
Unsuitable for the freezer

6–8 potatoes, 2 onions
2 medium leeks (white part only)
25g (1oz) butter
1 litre (1¾pt) good light stock
250ml (9fl oz) double cream
salt, pepper, chives

1 Cut onions and leeks into thin rings and sauté in butter in a saucepan on low heat for about 5 min. Do not allow to go brown.
2 Peel potatoes and cut in thin slices. Place in pan and add stock.
3 Cover, and leave soup to simmer until potatoes are tender.
4 Mash through a sieve or purée in a liquidizer. Bring soup back to the boil, and season to taste with salt and white pepper. Place soup in a cool place.
5 Stir in cream and a generous amount of chives.
Serve soup ice cold, with some melba toast.

Cold Spinach Soup

(serves 4)
Preparation time: about 20 min
Cooking time: 10–15 min
Unsuitable for the freezer

700g (1½lb) fresh spinach
225g (½lb) sorrel leaves (or more spinach)
225g (½lb) beetroot leaves
25g (1oz) butter
4 × 15ml tbsp (4tbsp) beetroot juice
1 × 15ml tbsp (1tbsp) vinegar
550ml (1pt) fish stock
400ml (¾pt) white wine
fennel, tarragon, salt, pepper

1 Chop the washed green leaves and sauté until tender in butter.
2 Rub mixture through a sieve or purée in a liquidizer. Add all the liquids, salt, pepper, herbs and a few ice cubes, and mix well. Cool before serving.
This soup goes beautifully with boiled salmon, sliced cucumber and grated fresh horseradish.

To make Tomato Soup as cold as possible, dilute with ice water and serve with ice cubes.

Cucumber Soup with Yoghurt

(serves 4)
Preparation time: about 10 min
Unsuitable for the freezer

1 large cucumber
salt, 2 cloves of garlic
600ml (just over 1pt) plain yoghurt
100g (4oz) walnuts
150ml ($\frac{1}{4}$pt) sour cream
finely chopped dill

1 Peel cucumber and cut into cubes. Sprinkle with a little salt, and leave in a cool place.
2 Crush the garlic and chop up the nuts.
3 Whisk together yoghurt and sour cream and add crushed garlic, chopped walnuts and drained cucumber cubes. Season soup to taste with salt and dill. Serve ice cold, with a couple of ice cubes in each plate if you like.

Yoghurt Soup

(serves 4)
Preparation time: 5–10 min
Unsuitable for the freezer

600ml (just over 1pt) plain yoghurt
250ml (9fl oz) skimmed milk
1 medium cucumber
2 × 5ml tsp (2tsp) salt
freshly ground white pepper
1 crushed clove of garlic
1$\frac{1}{2}$ × 15ml tbsp (1$\frac{1}{2}$tbsp) olive oil
$\frac{1}{2}$ × 5ml tsp ($\frac{1}{2}$tsp) dried tarragon, fresh dill

1 Peel cucumber and cut into small cubes.
2 Mix yoghurt and milk and stir in cucumber cubes. Season to taste with salt, pepper and herbs.
3 Sprinkle with olive oil and leave soup in the refrigerator for a couple of hours. Serve with or without ice cubes – but make sure it is ice cold.

Cold or Hot Carrot Soup with Caraway

(serves 4)
Preparation time: about 10 min
Cooking time: 10 min
Unsuitable for the freezer

250g (9oz) carrots
1 litre (1$\frac{3}{4}$pt) stock
200g (7oz) lettuce or Chinese cabbage
salt, pepper
$\frac{1}{2}$–1 × 5ml tsp ($\frac{1}{2}$–1tsp) caraway seeds
finely chopped parsley

1 Scrape, wash and roughly grate the carrots. Boil the stock and add the grated carrots and the sliced lettuce or Chinese cabbage.
2 Season to taste with salt, pepper and caraway seeds, and leave soup to simmer for about 10 min. Serve well chilled, or hot, with parsley.

Cucumber Soup

(serves 4)
Preparation time: about 15 min
Cooking time: 8–10 min
Unsuitable for the freezer

2 cucumbers
1 litre (1¾pt) chicken stock (or
*   cube + water)*
1 onion
15g (½oz) butter or 1 × 15ml tbsp
*   (1tbsp) oil*
100g (4oz) mushrooms
salt, freshly ground pepper
finely chopped chives

1 Peel the cucumbers and cut in half
lengthwise. Slice each half thinly,
and place in boiling stock. Simmer
on low heat for about 8 min.
2 Peel and roughly chop the onion.
Sauté until golden in butter together
with the cleaned, sliced mushrooms.
Season to taste with salt and pepper
and put mushrooms and onion into
the soup. Season with more spices if
necessary and place in a cool place.
Serve soup ice cold with lots of
finely chopped chives.

Courgette Soup (left)

(serves 4)
Preparation time: 10–15 min
Cooking time: 5 min
Unsuitable for the freezer

900g (2lb) courgettes
1 clove of garlic
700–900ml (1¼–1½pt) stock
grated nutmeg, butter
For the garnishes:
2 hard-boiled eggs
125g (4½oz) fresh mushrooms
1 × 15ml tbsp (1tbsp) lemon juice
8–10 radishes
French bread
butter, 2–3 cloves of garlic

1 Peel the courgettes and slice
finely.
2 Sauté crushed garlic in a little
butter, add stock and bring to the
boil. Leave to cool.
3 Purée courgette slices in a
liquidizer or mincer and add to the
cooled stock. Season to taste with
salt and grated nutmeg and leave
soup in the refrigerator for another
couple of hours.
4 While soup is chilling, make the
garnishes. Stir together soft butter
and crushed garlic or garlic powder
to taste. Slice the French bread and

spread garlic butter on each slice.
Place slices on a baking sheet and
leave in a hot oven for about 5 min.
Serve soup with the garlic bread,
and arrange dishes of coarsely chopped eggs, radishes and mushrooms
(sprinkled with lemon juice) on the
table so that everyone can help
themselves.

Thickened Cucumber Soup

(serves 4)
Preparation time: about 10 min
Cooking time: about 10 min
Unsuitable for the freezer

2 cucumbers, 1 onion
15g (½oz) butter
3 × 15ml tbsp (3tbsp) plain flour
700ml (1¼pt) stock
1 × 5ml tsp (1tsp) salt, black pepper
a pinch of grated nutmeg
100ml (4fl oz) double cream
1 egg yolk
1 bunch of chives

Both Yoghurt Soup (front) and
Cucumber Soup are delicious chilled.
Serve with bread or crispbread and
butter, and lots of dill or chives.

1 Peel cucumbers and grate them
roughly, keeping a small piece with
the peel on one side.
2 Finely chop the onion and sauté
until shiny in butter. Sprinkle in the
flour, then add stock slowly, and the
grated cucumber. Season to taste
with salt, pepper and nutmeg. Leave
soup to simmer for about 8–10 min.
3 Mix cream and egg yolk with a
dash of water and pour mixture into
soup pan. The soup must not be
brought to the boil after the egg yolk
have been added.
4 Chop the last piece of the cucumber roughly and finely chop the
chives. Stir both ingredients into the
soup and leave to cool.
Serve with white bread, butter and
cheese.

Imitation Borsch
(serves 4)
Preparation and cooking time: 15–20 min
Unsuitable for the freezer

1 litre (1¾pt) meat soup from can or packet
6 pickled beetroots
50 ml (2fl oz) beetroot brine
salt, pepper, lemon juice
sour cream

1 Prepare and heat the soup, following the instructions on the can or packet.
2 Slice beets into fine strips and place in the soup. Add beet brine'

and season soup to taste with salt, pepper and a dash of lemon juice. Serve with sour cream.

Avocado Soup
(serves 4–6)
Preparation time: about 20 min
Unsuitable for the freezer

4 avocados
400–550ml (¾–1pt) chicken stock
250ml (9fl oz) double cream
100ml (4fl oz) dry white wine
2 × 5ml tsp (2tsp) lemon juice
salt, pepper, cayenne pepper
chives or dill

1 Cut avocados in half. Remove

Avocado can be used in many ways. Here it is puréed for a delicious cold soup.

stones and peel.
2 Purée the avocado flesh with half the lemon juice in a liquidizer or push through a fine-meshed plastic sieve. Stir in the cream and white wine alternatively; beating well. Add a little more lemon juice, salt, pepper, and a pinch of cayenne (it's very strong).
3 Place a lid or tinfoil on top of the soup and chill in the refrigerator.
Serve the soup ice cold, with finely chopped dill or chives sprinkled on top.

Real Borsch

(serves 4–5)
Preparation time: about 15 min
Cooking time: about 1 hr, 15 min in all
Unsuitable for the freezer

5 large, raw beetroots
25–40g (1–1½oz) butter
1 × 15ml tbsp (1tbsp) vinegar
1 litre (1¾pt) good strong stock
salt, pepper, butter, sour cream

1 Clean and peel the beetroots. Grate roughly or slice finely.
2 Melt the butter and add beetroot and vinegar. Leave to simmer for about 20 min.
3 Add a little of the boiling stock and cook for a bit longer until the liquid has evaporated. Add some more stock and leave to simmer until the beets are tender.
4 Add the remaining stock and boil for about 30 min more.
5 Strain soup and season with salt and pepper. Stir in sour cream if you are serving the soup hot. For cold soups, place dollops of sour cream in each soup plate.

Sausage and Beetroot Soup

(serves 4)
Preparation time: about 15 min
Cooking time: 50–60 min in all
Unsuitable for the freezer

4–5 beetroots, salt
200g (7oz) cabbage, 1 onion
1.4 litres (2½pt) good strong stock
400g (14oz) small garlic or boiling
*   sausages*
150–200ml (5–7fl oz) sour cream

1 Wash beetroots thoroughly and boil until tender in lightly salted water. Rinse under cold, running water and rub off the peel.
2 Slice cabbage and onion thinly. Place in boiling stock and leave to simmer until tender. Slice beets into strips, place in soup with the sausage slices and boil for a further 5 min.
3 Season soup with salt and pepper. Stir in sour cream.

There are many recipes for beetroot soups from Russia. Above is a sophisticated, strained beetroot soup with dollops of sour cream – real Borsch – and below is the more filling Sausage and Beetroot Soup.

Berry Soup
about 450g (1lb) jam (strawberry,
  raspberry, or similar)
1 litre ($\frac{3}{4}$pt) water, sugar
1$\frac{1}{2}$ × 5ml tsp (1$\frac{1}{2}$tsp) potato flour,
  cornflour or arrowroot

Mix jam and water and bring to the
boil. Season with sugar if necessary.
Thicken with flour mixed with a
dash of cold water. Add less liquid
and extra thickening for a sauce to
serve with steamed puddings.

Lemon Soup (left)
2 lemons
1 litre (1$\frac{3}{4}$pt) water
1 × 15ml tbsp (1tbsp) potato flour,
  cornflour or arrowroot
sugar, 1 egg

1 Finely grate the rind of 1 lemon,
and roughly chop the peel of the
other. Squeeze the juice, then boil
juice and rind in 1 litre (1$\frac{3}{4}$pt) water.
Add sugar to taste, and cook until
rind is tender (5–6 min).
2 Mix flour with a little cold water
and whisk this thickening into the
soup. Remove pan from heat and
mix egg yolk with some of the hot
soup. Pour mixture back into the
soup and whisk well.
3 Whisk egg white until stiff and
place dollops of it into the soup just
before serving.

Fruit Soups

*Fruit and berry soups are an
unusual idea from
Scandinavia. They can be
served as a normal soup (if
not too sweet) or as a dessert.
With less liquid and a little
extra thickening the following
recipes can be adapted to
make interesting sauces to
serve hot with meat, fish or
puddings; or cold with ice
cream.*

Use fresh or tinned fruit, jam or
juice, fresh or frozen berries and
dried fruit. Potato flour is the
most common thickening. Allow
1$\frac{1}{2}$–2 × 15ml tbsp (1$\frac{1}{2}$–2tbsp) to
700–900ml (1$\frac{1}{4}$–1$\frac{1}{2}$pt) soup, which is
enough for 4. Mix the flour with a
little cold water and add to the boiling soup. Bring soup to the boil
again, stirring continuously, and
remove from the heat. Cornflour or
arrowroot can also be used as thick-
enings. Use the same amount of
flour but leave soup to simmer for
2–3 min after adding the thickening.
Sprinkle soup with a dash of sugar to
prevent a skin forming.

Apricot and/or Prune Soup

about 200g (7oz) dried fruit
1¼ litres (just over 2pt) water, sugar
1½–2 × 5ml tsp (1½–2tsp) potato
 flour, cornflour, or arrowroot

1 Rinse prunes and/or apricots well and soak in the cold water for a few hours.
2 Boil the fruit in the soaking water and add sugar to taste.
3 Stir flour in a little cold water and stir thickening into soup. Bring to the boil and remove saucepan from the heat.
Serve cold, with or without whipped cream. Alternatively, add less liquid and extra thickening and serve as a sauce with gammon.

Gooseberry Soup with Wine

450g (1lb) gooseberries
250ml (9fl oz) white wine
500ml (just under 1pt) water
200g (7oz) sugar
grated rind of ½ lemon
2 × 15ml tbsp (2tbsp) potato flour or
 arrowroot
a dash of rum (optional)

1 Clean berries and boil until tender in water and wine, along with lemon rind and most of the sugar.
2 Mix potato flour or arrowroot with a little cold water and stir into soup. Bring to the boil and remove saucepan from the heat.
Serve gooseberry soup cold with whipped cream. For a fresh, sharp sauce to serve with goose or mackerel, boil gooseberries in a small amount of water and wine, add 1 × 15ml tbsp (1tbsp) sugar and lemon rind and thickening as required.

Rosehip Soup

450g (1lb) fresh rose hips
1 litre (1¾pt) water
100g (4oz) sugar
1½ × 15ml tbsp (1½tbsp) potato flour
 or arrowroot

1 Boil rose hips in water till tender. Mash them and add more water if necessary (about 1 litre or 1¾pt mash in all).
2 Bring mash to the boil, season with sugar and thicken with potato flour or arrowroot mixed with a little cold water.
Serve rosehip soup with chopped almonds and whipped cream.

Gooseberry Soup with Wine is an unusual course with which to end a gourmet dinner.

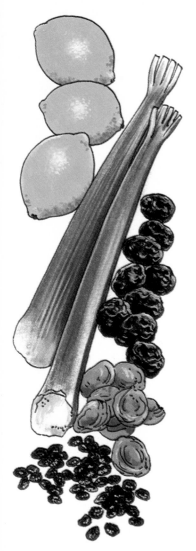

Index